T H E
BISMARCK

ROBERT JACKSON

THE
BISMARCK

ROBERT JACKSON

SPELLMOUNT
Staplehurst

British Library Cataloguing in Publication Data:
A catalogue record for this book is available
from the British Library

Copyright © Amber Books Ltd 2002

ISBN 1-86227-173-9

First published in the UK in 2002 by
Spellmount Ltd
The Old Rectory
Staplehurst
Kent TN12 0AZ

Tel: 01580 893730
Fax: 01580 893731
E-mail: enquiries@spellmount.com
Website: www.spellmount.com

1 3 5 7 9 8 6 4 2

Editorial and design: Amber Books Ltd
Bradley's Close, 74–77 White Lion Street,
London N1 9PF

Project Editor: Chris Stone
Design: Graham Curd

Printed and bound in The Slovak Republic

Picture credits

Blue Water Recoveries Limited / David Mearns: 82-83, 84, 85, 86, 87.
Robert Jackson: 37
Naval Historical Center, Washington: 22, 23, 33 (b), 48, 49.
Popperfoto: 38, 41, 59.
Süddeutscher Verlag: 20-21, 29, 34-35, 58.
TRH Pictures: 6-7, 8, 9, 10-11 (all), 12-13, 16-17 (all), 18, 19, 30 (b), 32, 33 (t),
36, 39, 42-43, 45, 46 (both), 47, 50-51, 51, 52, 54, 55, 56, 57, 60-61, 62-63
(both), 64-65 (all), 66, 67, 69, 70 (both), 71, 72 (both), 73, 74, 75, 76, 77 (both),
78, 79, 80, 81.
Private Collection: 26, 27 (both), 30 (t), 31, 50.

Illustrations by Amber Books Ltd and Aerospace Publishing.

CONTENTS

CHAPTER 1

A Fleet Reborn

By 1934, only fifteen years after the High Seas Fleet scuttled itself at Scapa Flow, the German Navy was again about to present a challenge.

The rise of Germany as a major naval power began in the latter years of the nineteenth century. It reached a pinnacle of strength in World War I, but withered away with the scuttling of the High Seas Fleet at Scapa Flow in June 1919. In the 1930s it witnessed a brief resurrection, only to vanish forever with the destruction of Nazi Germany's mighty capital ships in World War II. Until that event, Germany's shipyards produced the two most powerful battleships afloat, presenting an unparalleled threat to Britain's ocean lifelines.

The design, development and eventual deployment of these two mighty vessels, the *Bismarck* and the *Tirpitz*, represented the culmination of Germany's naval ambition. This first surfaced at the end of the twentieth century, at a time when France, Britain's ancient maritime adversary, was no longer in a position to challenge British naval supremacy. The new challenge came from Imperial Germany, and the man who threw down the gauntlet was Kaiser Wilhelm II himself, who had long been an admirer of British naval technology. Thanks to the Kaiser's patronage, Admiral Alfred von Tirpitz became the Secretary of State for the Reichsmarineamt, the leading administrative office of the Imperial German Navy. Having assumed this post on 15 June 1897, he saw his plans for the future German Navy mature very quickly, and in 1898 and 1900 these were approved by the Reichstag in two Naval Laws.

TWO-POWER STANDARD

Tirpitz justified the build-up of a modern German fleet by stressing that the defence of Germany would depend on the outcome of a naval battle in the North Sea. From this, he concluded that any German fleet must therefore be strong enough to confront even the British fleet, with all its overwhelming capital ship supremacy. Since the latter years of the eigtheenth century, Britain's naval policy had revolved around what was described as a 'two-power standard', which kept the Royal Navy equal in numbers to any two foreign navies. In 1889 the two-power standard was modified

The battlecruiser *Scharnhorst* under construction at the Wilhelmshaven Naval Dockyard in 1934. The warship was laid down as the 'D' or Ersatz Elsass (*Elsass* Replacement) and launched in October 1936.

somewhat when the Naval Defence Act came into force, decreeing that the Royal Navy must be capable of matching the world's second- and third-largest navies. The result was a new phase of shipbuilding, with the Royal Sovereign class of battleship at its forefront. A highly successful design, the Royal Sovereigns (of which there were eight) were faster than any contemporary battleships. Their main armament of four 343mm (13.5in) guns was mounted in twin barbettes; they also carried ten 152mm (6in) guns, 16 six-pounder guns and seven 45.7cm (18in) torpedo tubes. The barbette arrangement, which saved a great deal of weight, meant that the Royal Sovereigns were a deck higher than contemporary low freeboard battleships, and were far better seaboats. They displaced 14,377 tonnes (14,150 tons), carried a complement of 712, had a maximum speed of 16.5 knots and an endurance of 8746km (4720nm).

PRE-DREADNOUGHT

In the 1890s the Royal Navy, closely followed by other major naval powers, developed a new standard type of battleship later known as the 'Pre-dreadnought'. The first was the 12,548-tonne (12,350-ton) HMS *Renown* of 1892, but it was the Majestic class of 1893–4 that served as the pattern for battleship design for the next decade. Displacing 15,129 tonnes (14,890 tons), they were armed with four 305mm (12in), 12

Below: The *Rheinland* was a Nassau class dreadnought. Built by the Vulcan Shipyard at Stettin, she was launched in September 1908 and fought in the Battle of Jutland in 1915, where she was damaged.

152mm (6in), 16 76mm (12pdr) and 12 47mm (3pdr) guns, as well as five 457mm (18in) torpedo tubes. In all, 42 Pre-dreadnoughts were built for the Royal Navy up to 1904.

Tirpitz, therefore, had a formidable task ahead of him, and he rose to meet it energetically. Between 1889 and 1904, under the provisions of a series of Naval Acts, he persuaded the Reichstag to order the construction of 20 battleships, the first being four ships of the Brandenburg class. These displaced 10,174 tonnes (10,013 tons) and were armed with four 280mm (11in) guns mounted in centre-line turrets. Tirpitz, faced with some criticism over the massive expenditure involved, now appealed to the pride of the German people. The possession of a powerful battle fleet was a matter of national prestige; since Germany was becoming a major industrial nation, she must have a navy to match her economic capability. The fact that he was precipitating a naval arms race on an unprecedented scale seemed a matter of little consequence.

SUPER-BATTLESHIP

The real impetus for a naval arms race, however, was brought about by two revolutionary British designs. The first was a 'super-battleship' whose prototype was laid down by Portsmouth Dockyard in October 1905; it was constructed in great secrecy and in record time, the vessel being ready for initial sea trials a year and a day later. HMS *Dreadnought*, as the formidable new warship was named, was revolutionary in that she was armed with ten 305mm (12in) guns, two in each of five turrets centrally placed on the ship. (In fact, only

eight guns in the first of these ships could be fully brought to bear, but this was remedied in its successors.) From 1906 onwards a first-class battleship was to be a ship capable of firing ten heavy guns on either side. Thus a Dreadnought could engage one older vessel with a superiority of ten to four, or two with a superiority of ten to eight. As well as being the first battleship with main armament of a single calibre, *Dreadnought* was also the first with steam turbines and quadruple screws, machinery that gave her a top speed of 21 knots. She carried a crew of 697 and displaced 18,187 tonnes (17,900 tons).

The other revolutionary warship concept was the battlecruiser. Though nearly equal in armament to the new battleships, it was very much swifter, a ship designed to cruise ahead and scout for the main battle fleet and to be capable of overwhelming any conventional cruiser. In fact, the concept arose from the simple fact that existing armoured cruisers had evolved into ships so large and expensive that they had reached the end of their development potential.

The first ship of the new class was HMS *Inflexible*, completed in 1908. She carried eight 305mm (12in) guns and had a speed of 26 knots. Her firepower was four-fifths that of a dreadnought, but a lot had to be sacrificed in the cause of speed. While the indicated horsepower of the *Dreadnought* was 18,000, that of the *Inflexible* was 41,000, so a large hull was needed to accommodate the necessary 31 boilers. With a reduced armament, and protection sacrificed for speed, the battlecruisers were inevitably more vulnerable, as was to be revealed at Jutland in 1916, when three were sunk.

BATTLECRUISERS

In 1908, the Germans passed yet another of their Navy Acts, making provision for an increase in the number of heavy warships. The 'large cruisers' that were the outcome of an earlier Navy Act, that of 1900, were now reclassified as battlecruisers, so that the planned combined battleship and battlecruiser strength envisaged for the Imperial German Navy over the coming years rose to 58 ships. Germany's first dreadnought-type battleships were the four vessels of the Nassau class, initiated in 1906. Shorter and wider than the British *Dreadnought*, and less heavily armed, they were nevertheless well protected and well armed: main armament comprised 12 280mm (11in) guns, with a secondary armament of 12 150 mm (5.9in). The disposition of the main armament, however, was poor, with broadside fire being restricted by the positioning of two turrets on each side amidships and one each fore and aft. The Heligoland class of 1908 were enlarged Nassaus with 305mm (12in) guns. They were the only German dreadnoughts with three funnels. They were marginally faster than the Nassaus – 20 knots against 19 – and displaced 23,166 tonnes (22,800 tons). Complement was 1100. They were followed by the Kaiser class of 1909–10; these were the first German battleships with turbine engines (built, ironically, by Parsons of Tyneside) and with a superfiring turret, mounted aft. The *Friedrich der Grosse*, launched in 1912, was designated flagship of the High Seas Fleet, and was to remain as such until 1917.

German capital ship building continued unabated in the years leading up to the outbreak of war in 1914. After the Kaiser class of dreadnoughts came the König class of 1911, the first German battleships to have all turrets mounted on the centreline; and the Baden class of 1913, two of which were never completed. The Badens were modified Königs, carrying a main armament of eight 381mm (15in) guns.

Above: Laid down by Vulcan as the Ersatz Heimdall in January 1910, the *Friedrich der Grosse* was a Kaiser-class battleship. Interned at Scapa Flow in 1918, she was scuttled there in June the following year.

MAJOR NAVAL BATTLE

At the beginning of World War I, Germany's military and naval planners were convinced that a land war on the continent could be won quickly and decisively, and that Britain would therefore be forced into a major naval battle in the North Sea, somewhere between Heligoland and the Thames Estuary. Contrary to expectations, however, the land war on the Western Front degenerated into static trench warfare, and it was not until 31 May 1916 that the British Grand Fleet and the German High Seas Fleet came into direct confrontation at the Battle of Jutland. During this massive engagement, which involved 259 warships, the Royal Navy lost more warships and men than the Germans, but gained a strategic victory in that the High Seas Fleet retreated to its main base at Wilhelmshaven and never ventured out in strength again.

For more than two years after the battle, the principal units of the German Fleet lay idle. Only in October 1918, as the war drew to its inevitable conclusion, did the German admirals plan to emerge for a fight to the finish in the North Sea. This suicidal scheme provoked open mutiny on the German warships at Kiel and Wilhelmshaven. Then, on 21 November 1918, ten days after the signing of the Armistice, the main body of the German High Seas Fleet, comprising nine battleships, five battlecruisers, seven light cruisers and 49 destroyers, sailed under escort from its North German bases to surrender to the Allies at Scapa Flow, the Royal Navy's anchorage in the Orkney Islands. There the warships and their crews languished, cut off from the outside world and receiving only basic rations and scanty communications from Germany, while an 'interim' German Navy was established in April 1919 under the command of Vice-Admiral von Trotha.

SCUTTLED

The future of the German High Seas Fleet was to have been agreed by the Allied and German delegations at Versailles, where a peace treaty was being negotiated. When the deadline for the decision arrived on 21 June 1919, the German warships at Scapa Flow were scuttled by their crews on the orders of Admiral von Reuter. Only the battleship *Baden* and a few destroyers were saved by British boarding parties. It was the end of the Imperial German Navy.

Only a week after the fleet scuttled itself at Scapa Flow, the Versailles Peace Treaty was formalized. As far as the German Navy was concerned, its restrictions were little

Below: Major surface units of the German High Seas Fleet pictured shortly after their arrival at Scapa Flow naval anchorage in the Orkney Islands on 28 November 1918.

short of draconian. In fact, when the Allies demanded the surrender of further capital ships to compensate for those scuttled at Scapa Flow, the German Navy was reduced to a coastal defence force, armed with a motley collection of obsolete warships that included eight old pre-war battleships. If new capital ships were built in the future to replace old vessels, their displacement was not to exceed 10,160 tonnes (10,000 tons), while that of new-build cruisers was to be no greater than 6096 tonnes (6000 tons).

In October 1920 Admiral von Trotha was replaced by Admiral Paul Behnke, whose priority was to restructure the Reichsmarine and train a future generation of naval officers. To this end, the government made funds available for the start of a modest shipbuilding programme, and also for refitting some of the old Imperial Navy warships. The battleships *Braunschweig*, *Elsass*, *Hannover* and *Hessen* were all refitted and rearmed in the early 1920s, while two others, *Schlesien* and *Schleswig-Holstein*, were reconstructed at a later date. In the late 1920s, the Reichsmarine, now under the command of Admiral Hans Zenker, found itself in the middle of a political storm when the German Socialist Party discovered that plans were being laid to build a new class of warship. Known initially as Panzerkreuzer (armoured cruisers) and later as Panzerschiffe (armoured ships), they were designed from the start as commerce raiders, with a large and economical radius of action of 16,677km (9,000nm) at 19 knots. In order to comply with the maximum tonnage specified by the various naval treaties of the 1920s, they were electrically welded to save weight and equipped with diesel engines. They had enough speed – 26 knots – to enable them to escape from any vessel that could not be overwhelmed by their guns. Their armament comprised six 28cm (11in), eight 15cm (5.9in), six 10.4cm (4.1in) AA, eight 37mm (1.44in) AA,

Above: The German commerce raider *Emden*, battered into a wreck by the cruiser HMAS *Sydney*, beached at North Keeling in the Cocos Islands in November 1914.

ten (later 28) 20mm (0.79in) AA guns and eight 53cm (21in) torpedo tubes. They carried a complement of 1150.

COMMERCE RAIDERS

Such was the weight of public opinion against the cost involved in building these warships that Admiral Zenker was replaced by an officer who was considered to be more acceptable to all political parties: Admiral Erich Raeder, who had left the Training Department in 1924 to become head of the Baltic Station, one of the three top positions in the Reichsmarine. Raeder had served as a staff officer to Admiral Franz von Hipper towards the end of World War I and had

later been assigned the task of writing two volumes of the official German history of the war at sea, a work he completed while in hiding in the Naval Historical Library following an accusation that he had been involved in the Navy-backed Berlin uprising of 1920. It was only while compiling this account that Raeder became fully aware of the activities of the German commerce raiders in distant waters during the war, and learned of the damage these vessels had inflicted on Allied shipping. Not only that – they had also tied down large numbers of Allied capital ships and cruisers, diverted to search for them.

The first of the new armoured ships, known initially as Schiff A or Ersatz Preussen, was laid down by Deutsche Werke, Kiel, on 5 February 1929. (The *Preussen*, the battleship she was to replace, as indicated by her designation, was stricken in April 1929 and scrapped in 1931). The new warship displaced 11,888 tonnes (11,700 tons) and was officially named *Deutschland* at her launch on 19 May 1931. A second vessel in the class was laid down at Wilhelmshaven as the Ersatz Lothringen on 25 June 1931 and was launched on 1 April 1933, receiving the name *Admiral Scheer*. A third, laid down at Wilhelmshaven on 1 October 1932 as the Ersatz Braunschweig, was named *Admiral Graf Spee* at her launch on 30 June 1934. There is little doubt that more of these fast, efficient 'pocket battleships' would have been ordered had not a change of naval policy followed the rise to power of Hitler and the National Socialist German Labour Party (NSDAP) in 1933.

NAVAL TREATIES

The rebirth of the German Navy took place against a background of, and for the time being outside the orbit of, a series of international naval treaties, the first of which was the Washington Naval Treaty, signed on 6 February 1922. The principal aim of the Washington Treaty, which was sponsored by the United States and which in effect was the first disarmament treaty in history, was to limit the size of the navies of the five principal maritime powers – at that time, Britain, the USA, France, Italy and Japan. For Britain, this meant a reduction in capital ship assets to twenty by scrapping existing warships and dropping new projects; however, because her capital ships were older and less heavily armed than those of the United States, she was permitted to build two new vessels as replacements for existing ones. The other nations were permitted to build new capital ships to replace vessels that were 20 years old. This arrangement would allow France and Italy to lay down new warships in 1927, while Britain, the USA and Japan would not need to do so until 1931. No new capital ship was to exceed 35,561 tonnes (35,000 tons), or mount guns larger than 41cm (16in). No existing capital ship was to be rebuilt, although an increase in deck armour against air attack was allowed, as was the addition of anti-torpedo bulges, provided these modifications did not exceed a total of 3048 tonnes (3000) tons.

Above: The battleship *Schleswig-Holstein* was one of three pre-dreadnoughts that Germany was permitted to retain under the terms of the Treaty of Versailles. All were rearmed in the 1920s.

By 1930, all the construction programmes of the maritime powers had been severely affected by economic constraints, the world being in the grip of a savage depression. With the exception of Japan, all the maritime nations were eager to escape the cost of building replacement capital ships, as permitted by the Washington Treaty, and on 22 April 1930 a new treaty, signed in London, made fresh provisions. Britain, Japan and the USA agreed that they would lay down no new capital ships before 1936, while France and Italy decided to lay down

only the two they were already allowed. Furthermore, the first three countries agreed to make further reductions in existing assets; Britain would reduce her force of capital ships to 15 by scrapping HMS *Tiger* and three Iron Duke-class vessels, and relegating the old *Iron Duke* herself to the role of training and depot ship. The United States and Japan also agreed to reduce their capital ship assets to fifteen and nine respectively.

NAVAL PARITY

Within three years, the Treaties of Washington and London had been torn to shreds by the march of international events. First of all, in 1933, Japan invaded Manchuria, giving notice to the world that she intended to establish domination of the Far East. She then withdrew from the League of Nations and quickly followed this step with a notice to end her adherence to the Washington and London Treaties, her intention being to establish naval parity with Britain and the USA. France, increasingly alarmed by the growing hostility of Fascist Italy, followed suit early in 1935. Also in 1935, and in defiance of the League of Nations, Italy embarked upon a campaign of aggression in Abyssinia; and in 1936, Germany, having repudiated the Treaty of Versailles, seized the Rhineland.

The Nazi Party had now been in power in Germany for several years, and one of the first acts of the new Chancellor, Adolf Hitler, was to initiate a massive rearmament programme. In the years between 1933 and 1937 the overall

The *Admiral Graf Spee*

The *Gneisenau*

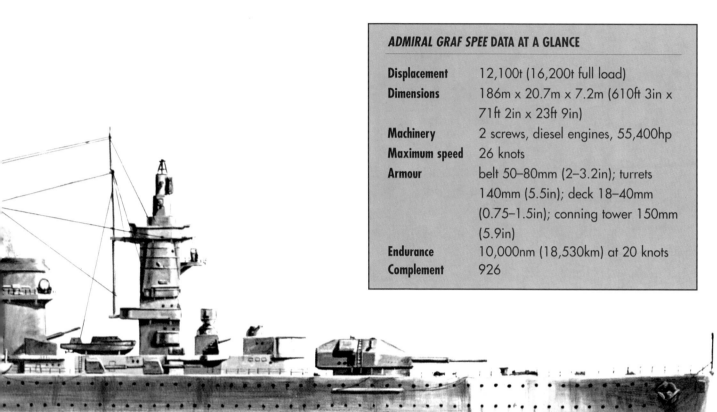

ADMIRAL *GRAF SPEE* DATA AT A GLANCE

Displacement	12,100t (16,200t full load)
Dimensions	186m x 20.7m x 7.2m (610ft 3in x 71ft 2in x 23ft 9in)
Machinery	2 screws, diesel engines, 55,400hp
Maximum speed	26 knots
Armour	belt 50–80mm (2–3.2in); turrets 140mm (5.5in); deck 18–40mm (0.75–1.5in); conning tower 150mm (5.9in)
Endurance	10,000nm (18,530km) at 20 knots
Complement	926

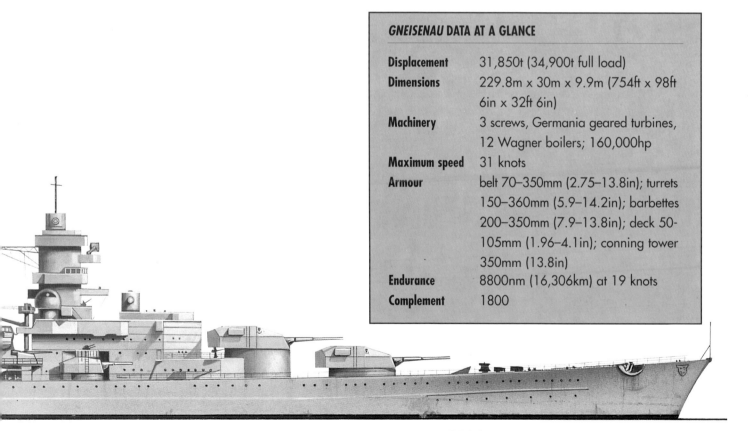

GNEISENAU DATA AT A GLANCE

Displacement	31,850t (34,900t full load)
Dimensions	229.8m x 30m x 9.9m (754ft x 98ft 6in x 32ft 6in)
Machinery	3 screws, Germania geared turbines, 12 Wagner boilers; 160,000hp
Maximum speed	31 knots
Armour	belt 70–350mm (2.75–13.8in); turrets 150–360mm (5.9–14.2in); barbettes 200–350mm (7.9–13.8in); deck 50–105mm (1.96–4.1in); conning tower 350mm (13.8in)
Endurance	8800nm (16,306km) at 19 knots
Complement	1800

Above: Admiral Erich Raeder, Commander-in-Chief of the Kriegsmarine during World War II. He was sentenced to life imprisonment at Nuremberg, but was released in 1955. He died in 1960.

Above: Captain Hans Langsdorff welcoming Adolf Hitler on board the 'pocket battleship' *Admiral Graf Spee*. A chivalrous officer, Langsdorff treated captured Allied merchant seaman with the utmost courtesy.

strategy of the Reichsmarine (renamed Kriegsmarine from 21 May 1935) changed from one of pure defence to one involving offensive operations in the Atlantic, France now being regarded as the main potential enemy. Hitler took an enormous interest in naval affairs, and displayed an amazing depth of knowledge of naval technology, gleaned from textbooks. He considered a strong battleship force essential, both as a tool to carry out his aggressive naval policy and as a strong lever in international politics. An immediate result of the policy shift was the construction of a new class of Schlachtkreuzer (Battlecruiser). Five ships were projected, but only two were started. The first of these, the 32,514-tonne (32,000-ton) *Scharnhorst*, was laid down at Wilhelmshaven in April 1934; she was followed a year later by the *Gneisenau*.

BEST CONTEMPORARY BATTLECRUISER

The design of these powerful warships was based on that of the uncompleted Mackensen class battlecruisers of World

War I, which in turn were based on the *Derfflinger* of 1912 – arguably the best battlecruiser of its day. The new ships were fitted with three-shaft geared turbines and their radius of action was 18,530km (10,000nm) at 19 knots. Their armament comprised nine 28cm (11in), 12 15cm (5.9in), 14 10.5cm (4.1in), 16 37mm (1.44in) AA, and ten (later 38) 20mm (0.78in) AA guns, as well as six 53cm (21in) torpedo tubes. Each carried four 'spotter' aircraft and had a complement of 1800. They were capable of a speed of 31 knots. *Scharnhorst* was launched in October 1936 and *Gneisenau* in December that year.

In the mid-1930s a new class of Schwerer Kreuzer (heavy cruiser) was also laid down. There were five ships in all, named *Lützow*, *Seydlitz*, *Prinz Eugen*, *Blücher* and *Admiral Hipper*. The first of these, launched in July 1939, was sold in

Right: The *Graf Spee*'s heavily armoured conning tower, taken by a US Navy photographer while the ship lay in Montevideo harbour. The Americans and British were interested in the warship's gunlaying radar.

1940 to the Soviet Navy, in whose service she was successively named *Petropavlovsk* and *Tallinn*. The others were all launched in 1937–39. Capable of 32 knots, their armament comprised eight 20cm (8in), twelve 10.5cm (4.1in) AA, twelve 37mm (1.44in) AA, and eight (later 28) 20mm (0.78in) AA guns, in addition to twelve 53cm (21in) torpedo tubes. Each carried three spotter aircraft. Complement was 1600.

In the late 1930s, German naval strategy still revolved around the possibility of a future conflict in the Atlantic, and the Munich Crisis of 1938 led Hitler to believe that there was now the prospect of a naval confrontation with Britain. To be assured of naval supremacy on the high seas, he needed a fleet of super-powerful battleships, two of which had already been laid down in 1936. These were the *Bismarck* and the *Tirpitz*, respectively laid down as Schiff F Ersatz Hannover and Schiff G Ersatz Schleswig-Holstein. Displacing 42,370 tonnes (41,700 tons) in the case of the *Bismarck* and 43,589 tonnes (42,900 tons) in the case of the *Tirpitz*, they would have a speed of 29 knots and a combat radius of 16,677km (9000nm) at 19 knots. They would carry a formidable armament of eight 38cm (15in), 12 15cm (5.9in), 16 10.5cm (4.1in) AA, 16 37mm (1.44in) AA and 16 (later 58) 20mm (0.78in) AA guns, together with eight 53cm (21in) torpedo tubes. Their complement would be 2400 officers and men. Six even larger (57,100-tonne/56,200-ton) battleships were planned, known simply by the letters H, J, K, L, M and N. Only H and J were laid down, in 1938, and these were broken up

on the stocks in the summer of 1940, at a time when Germany believed she had won the war.

Even more ambitious was a project to build several battleships of 111,765 tonnes (110,000 tons), which was quite beyond the capability of any shipbuilder anywhere in the world. There was even a scheme, known as the H44 Study, that envisaged a massive warship of 143,770 tonnes (141,500 tons), based on the H Class design and mounting a main armament of 50.8cm (20in) guns. Such a fantasy showed, as was also demonstrated in the future development of German 'secret weapons' such as jet and rocket aircraft and atomic weapons, how far the ambitions of Germany's scientists reached.

'POCKET' BATTLESHIPS

Admiral Raeder knew that the only chance of defeating Britain quickly was by severing her ocean lifelines, which meant extensive commerce raiding on the high seas. This was to be accomplished by long-range warships – 'pocket' battleships, battlecruisers and heavy cruisers – operating singly at first, and replenishing at sea from supply vessels. Later, these lone raiders were to be joined by integrated task forces, at the heart of which would be either one of the new super-powerful battleships or a battlecruiser, supported by a heavy cruiser and an aircraft carrier.

In the late 1930s, Germany had plans to build a small number of aircraft carriers; in the event there was only one, the 23,370-tonne (23,200-ton) *Graf Zeppelin*, laid down in 1936 and launched in December 1938. Her four-shaft geared turbines would have given her a maximum speed of 33 knots and a combat radius of 14,824km (8000nm) at 19 knots. It was originally planned that she should carry an air group comprising 12 Junkers Ju 87D dive bombers and 30 Messerschmitt Bf 109 fighters, later amended to 28 Ju 87s and 12 Me109s. She was never completed. (The air group intended for her, 4/Trägergruppe 186, was in fact used against shipping in the Baltic during the invasion of Poland in September 1939.) Construction was suspended in May 1940 when she was 85 per cent complete; she was afterwards towed to Gdynia and then to Stettin. In 1942 she went to Kiel, where work on her was restarted; it was again suspended in 1943, after which she was towed to the

Left: The German battlecruiser *Derfflinger* was probably the best warship design to emerge from World War I. She is seen here with battle damage from Jutland.

Above: The damaged battlecruiser *Seydlitz* pictured in Wilhelmshaven after being severely damaged by 23 shell hits and torpedoes at the Battle of Jutland. She lost 98 men.

Oder River and scuttled near Stettin in April 1945. In March 1946 she was raised by the Russians and towed to Swinemunde. In September 1947 she struck a mine and either sank north of Danzig, or was towed to Leningrad, severely damaged, and was broken up there.

The hull of a sister vessel was completed up to the armoured deck but she was never launched, being broken up on the stocks in 1940. It is possible that this ship was to have been named Peter Strasser, after the commander of the German Naval Airship Division in World War I. In 1942 work was also started to convert the heavy cruiser *Seydlitz* as an aircraft carrier, but very little was completed and the ship was scuttled at Königsberg in April 1945, later being raised by the Russians. Plans were also laid to convert the liners *Europa*, *Gneisenau* and *Potsdam* as an emergency measure, but these came to nothing.

BATTLESHIP CONSTRUCTION

In March 1939, however, aircraft carriers still featured prominently in the Germany Navy's scheme of things. On 1 March, the German leadership adopted the final draft of the so-called Z-Plan, which had been formulated in the first place to

accommodate the new battleship construction demanded by Hitler and which had undergone a number of modifications in the interim. The final Z-Plan envisaged four aircraft carriers, eight battleships, five battlecruisers, eight heavy cruisers (this figure including the 'pocket' battleships) and many smaller vessels, including 249 submarines; all the vessels enumerated in the plan were to remain in commission until 1948. Unfortunately, the plan took little account of the fact that the naval construction programme was already causing an acute shortage of strategic materials, in particular high-grade steel, and a drain on dockyard personnel resources that was fast becoming unacceptable.

Nevertheless, the re-arming of the German Navy appeared to be proceeding smoothly, despite inter-service rivalry over the distribution of funds and the exercise of control. (Hermann Göring, the Luftwaffe Commander-in-Chief, was adamant that all aircraft, even those on aircraft carriers, should remain his responsibility.) The new construction programmes had been accelerated on the orders of Hitler himself, but in the spring of 1939, with the Munich crisis over and Britain, France and the United States making no more than protests about Germany's invasion of Czechoslovakia, there did not seem to be any particular sense of urgency. Although a war with Great Britain was thought to be inevitable in the long run, the German Navy's leadership did not expect to have to fight it before 1944.

CHAPTER 2

Bismarck and *Tirpitz*: Design and Development

By the late 1930s, Germany's capital ships were among the most powerful in the world. It took all the Royal Navy's resources to hunt them down.

On 20 June 1935, an Anglo-German Agreement was signed. Under its terms, German warship tonnage was restricted to 35 per cent of British equivalents of all classes except submarines, which could be built up to 45 per cent. In effect, this meant that Germany could legitimately build U-boats up to a total of 24,385 tonnes (24,000 tons). At this time, the Royal Navy had 59 submarines in commission, of which 20 were in the 1372–1,834 tonne (1350–1805 ton) range; the rest were between 416 and 680 tonnes (410 and 670 tons), which was about the size the Germans were planning. The Agreement was concluded without consultation with the Dominions, France or the United States, and it is not clear why it was signed at all, unless the British Admiralty mistakenly believed that it would lead to the Germans building 45 per cent of the British total in numbers rather than in tonnage, which would have resulted in only 26 U-boats. What it actually did was to open the door for a massive increase in Germany's submarine fleet, because 12 254-tonne (250-ton) U-boats had already been laid down before the Agreement was signed and 12 more were to be added during the year.

DESIGN FEATURES

Another factor leading to a huge increase in the size of Germany's submarine fleet was the Anglo–German Naval Agreement (which was repudiated completely by Adolf Hitler on 28 April 1939). This also gave the green light for the construction of the two new battleships, Schiff F Ersatz Hannover and Schiff G Ersatz Schleswig-Holstein, later to be named *Bismarck* and *Tirpitz*. The former was ordered almost immediately after the signing of the Agreement, and preliminary design work was completed five months later, on 16

Left: The battleship *Bismarck* is launched on 14 February 1939 by Dorothea von Löwenfeld, Bismarck's grand-daughter. Adolf Hitler, Hermann Göring and Rudolph Hess are among those in attendance.

November 1935. It has often been claimed that the design of the two battleships was based on that of the Baden class of World War I, laid down in 1916 as a reply to the British Queen Elizabeth class. In fact, the only design features the two classes had in common were their armament, comprising eight 38cm (15in) guns in four twin turrets, and a three-shaft propulsion plant. It is more accurate to say that the two warships were improved and enlarged versions of the *Scharnhorst* and the *Gneisenau*, many of whose features they incorporated.

To build Schiff F, the Reichsmarineamt selected the very experienced Hamburg firm of Blohm & Voss. Founded in 1877 by Hermann Blohm and Ernst Voss, the firm had been responsible for some notable capital ship designs, including the battlecruisers *Goeben* and *Derfflinger*, and the incomplete Mackensen class of 1915. The task of building Schiff G, on the other hand, was assigned to the Wilhelmshaven Naval Dockyard. Schiff F's keel was laid on 1 July 1936 on slipway 9 in yard No. BV509; that of Schiff G on 24 October the same year. Work proceeded at a steady pace; by September 1938 the hull was already complete to the level of the upper deck. The ship originally had a straight stem, but this was changed to an 'Atlantic' or clipper bow after launching. Before this modification, the battleship had an overall length of 248m (814ft), reducing to 240.2m (788.3ft) at the waterline; her beam was an impressive 36m (118ft 2in) and draught was 10.2m (33ft 9in). With the modified bow, overall length became 251m (823ft).

ARMOUR AND ENGINES

Protection was a key factor in the battleship's design, and the result was a vessel capable of absorbing a tremendous

Above: After her launch, *Bismarck* is towed to the equipping pier to be fitted out. The hull was completed and the machinery installed, but months of work lay ahead before she was finished.

amount of damage. The hull was subdivided into 22 watertight compartments, numbered in sequence from stern to bows; this arrangement closely followed that of the Baden, although the major compartments were larger than those of Baden to obviate the problems of cramped conditions, especially in the engine rooms. No less than 70 per cent of the waterline length was protected by heavy armour that included a long anti-torpedo bulge. Several new materials were used in the armour composition, virtually doubling the efficiency of anything available previously; the most important were 'Wotan Weich' (WW), which was designed to absorb shell impacts, and 'Wotan Hart' (Wh), which had the ability to deflect missiles. Another protective material was Krupp Cementit (KC), 100mm (4in) of which was equivalent to 80mm (3.25in) of Wotan Weich and 60mm (2.25in) of Wotan Hart. The lower main belt of the warship had a thickness of 320mm (12.75in), reduced to 315mm (12.5in) in the *Tirpitz*), and together with an armoured deck that had a thickness of between 110 and 120mm (4.25–4.5in), this made the *Bismarck* the best-protected warship in the world. Her designers were confident that she could resist any projectile, fired from whatever range, and that she would be practically immune in close-range engagements, where shells would not have the penetrating power that they did at long range, where they entered high ballistic trajectories.

Both the *Bismarck* and the *Tirpitz* were fitted with Brown-Boveri geared turbines; there were three engine rooms, one astern and serving the middle shaft, while two others amidships served the port and starboard shafts. Twelve Wagner boilers were fitted. Each screw had a diameter of 4.85m (16ft) and produced 2825 revolutions per minute at maximum speed, reducing to 2390 revolutions per minute at cruising speed. Twin rudders were installed, each with a surface area of 24m² (29 yards²). The ships' bunkers had a maximum capacity for 8000 tonnes (7872 tons) of fuel oil, although 4000 tonnes (3936 tons) was the more normal load.

With the hull complete and main machinery installed, the launching ceremony took place on Tuesday 14 February 1939, and was attended by thousands of people. After a speech by Adolf Hitler, the ship was launched by Frau Dorothea von Löwenfeld, granddaughter of the Prussian statesman and first chancellor of the German Empire, Prince Otto Eduard Leopold von Bismarck Schönhausen (1815–98). After launching, the ship was moored to the equipping pier, where the work of fitting her out began.

ARMAMENT

The *Bismarck*'s main armament comprised eight 38cm (15in) L/47 guns, constructed in 1934; the barrel weight was 109.2 tonnes (107 tons); projectile weight 798kg (1760lb); muzzle velocity 850m/sec (2788ft/sec); and rate of fire per barrel three rounds per minute. Each gun was supplied with between 105 and 120 rounds. Maximum elevation was 35 degrees, at which a projectile could be hurled 36,200m (22.5 miles). The barrels needed to be changed after 200 rounds had been fired. The main armament was installed in two pairs of superfiring turrets, fore and aft, each weighing 1000

tonnes (984 tons), named Anton, Berta, Cäsar and Dora.

Secondary armament consisted of 12 15.2cm (6in) L/55 guns, 1928 model; these had a barrel weighing 9.1 tonnes (89.5 tons), and fired a projectile weighing 43.3kg (97lb). Muzzle velocity was 850m/sec (2788ft/sec) and rate of fire per barrel 10 rounds per minute. Each gun was supplied with 150 rounds. Range at maximum elevation of 35 degrees was 22,000m (13.6 miles). A barrel change was needed after 2500 rounds had been fired. The secondary armament was installed in three twin turrets to port and starboard.

Anti-aircraft armament comprised 16 10.5cm (4in) L/65 guns, 1932 model; these fired a projectile weighing 15.1kg (40lb) and had a muzzle velocity of 880m/sec (2886ft/sec). Rate of fire per barrel was 12–15 rounds per minute, and each gun was supplied with 420 rounds of ammunition. Range at maximum elevation of 44 degrees was 17,700m (11 miles) and the gun had a maximum effective altitude of 12,800m (42,000ft). A barrel change was needed after 3500 rounds had been fired. The 10.5s were installed in twin mountings on the boat deck and to port and starboard.

Anti-aircraft armament also included 16 L/83 37mm semi-automatic guns, 1930 model, which fired a shell weighing 745g (1.7lb); muzzle velocity was 1000m/sec (3280ft/sec) and rate of fire per barrel of 30 rounds per minute. Each gun had a supply of 2000 rounds. Maximum elevation was 44 degrees, giving a range of 8500m (5.2 miles), and maximum-

Below: *Bismarck*'s secondary armament of twelve 15.2cm (6in) guns was installed in twin turrets, three to port and three to starboard. Each gun was supplied with 150 rounds of ammunition.

The *Prinz Eugen*

effective altitude was 6800m (19,680ft). The guns were installed in eight twin mountings. Finally, there were 12 20mm guns, 1930 model; these had a muzzle velocity of 840m/sec (2755ft/sec), a maximum effective altitude of 400m (1312ft) and were installed in single mountings.

OPTICAL EXCELLENCE

Both the *Bismarck* and the *Tirpitz* were equipped with Seetakt radar, each vessel being fitted with two sets. Since 1934, the Kriegsmarine had shown keen interest in the devel-

opment of radar equipment by GEMA, a company specifically established for research into radiolocation techniques, and from 1938–39 several German capital ships were fitted with Seetakt, which worked on the 80cm (31.5in) wavelength. At the outbreak of war Seetakt was standard equipment in the larger German warships, identifiable by its large antenna, nicknamed 'mattress' by the Germans and installed in front of the rangefinder cupolas. Seetakt was quite useful for navigation and search purposes, yet the Germans made little tactical use of it, being convinced that the British had developed effective

THE *BISMARCK* DATA AT A GLANCE			
Displacement	45,172t standard; 50,900t full load	**Armament**	eight 38cm (15in); 12 15cm(5.9in);
Dimensions	248 x 36 x 10.6m (813ft 8in x 118ft 1in x 34ft 9in)		16 10.5cm (4.1in); 16 37mm; 12 20mm; 4–6 Arado Ar 196 aircraft
Machinery	three-shaft Brown-Boveri (Blohm & Voss) geared turbines, 138,000hp (150,170hp achieved on trials)	**Complement**	103 officers, 1962 ratings, 27 marines (boarding party)
		Weight Distribution	Hull: 12,700t (25.4%)
Speed	29 knots (31.1 knots achieved on trials)		Armour: 17,256t (38.2%)
		Engine installations	2756t (6.1%)
Range	15,750km (8500nm) at 19 knots	**Auxiliary motors**	1400t (3.1%)
Armour	belt 318mm–267mm (12.5in–10.5in);	**Armament**	1345t (3.0%)
	deck 121mm–51mm (4.75in–2in);	**Fuel**	3388t (7.5%)
	main turrets 362mm–178mm (14.5in–7in);	**Catapult and associated aircraft equipment**	100t (0.2%)
	secondary turrets 102mm–37mm (4in–1.5in);	**Construction costs**	approx 196.8 million Reichsmarks (about £9.4 million at 1939 rates)
	conning tower 356mm (14in)	**Time in service**	277 days. Operational life: 215 hours

Above: After the loss of the *Bismarck* the heavy cruiser *Prinz Eugen* made for the port of Brest, where she remained until she escaped in the famous 'Channel Dash' of February 1942.

methods of detecting radar transmissions. So, instead of developing what was already superior naval radar equipment, German scientists concentrated on the development of their own radar detection devices.

This mistake also placed great reliance on the warships' superb stereoscopic optical rangefinding equipment, which was incredibly accurate, especially at initial ranges. Whereas a German operator only had to centre his little yellow 'wandermark' at the base of an enemy ship's superstructure, a British operator, using a coincidental rangefinder, had to merge two images into one. The ranges (visual, supported ocasionally by radar) were fed by electric circuits to computers in transmitting stations deep within the ship, togeth-

er with the course and speed of both attacker and target vessel, wind velocity, air density, rate of range change, and so on. Searchlights were also fitted for target illumination.

SPOTTER AIRCRAFT

One notable feature of the *Bismarck* was the large aircraft hangar, situated midships aft of the funnel and housing up to six Arado Ar 196 floatplanes behind a massive watertight sliding door. The twin-float Ar 196 was designed as a successor to the Heinkel He 50, a catapult-launched spotter biplane carried by German warships in the 1930s; it first flew in the summer of 1938 and 536 Ar 196A production aircraft were built, entering service shortly before the outbreak of World War II. The major production model was the Ar 196A-3, one of which became famous on 5 May 1940 by accepting the surrender of HM submarine *Seal*, which had been forced to the surface in the Kattegat with mine damage. As the specifi-

THE *PRINZ EUGEN* DATA AT A GLANCE			
Displacement	16,974t standard, 19,042t full load		main turrets 17cm–5.7cm (6.7–2.24in),
Dimensions	199.50 x 21.50 x 6.60m (654ft 6in x 70ft 6in x 21ft 8in)		conning tower 15.2cm–5.0cm (6in–2in)
Machinery	three shafts, Brown-Boveri geared turbines, 9 La Mont boilers; 132,000hp	Armament	Eight 203mm (8in) 60/C34 main armament in four superfiring two-gun turrets fore and aft; 12 37mm
Max speed	32.5 knots		in six twin-gun mountings; eight
Range	12,600km (6800nm) at 20 knots		20mm AA; 12 533mm (21 inch)
Armour	belt 8.2cm–3.8cm (3.32–1.5in), deck 3.1cm–1.27cm (1.22–0.5in), torpedo bulkhead 1.90cm (0.75in),		torpedo tubes; three Ar 196 aircraft
		Complement	1600

THE ARADO AR 196 DATA AT A GLANCE

Crew	2	Height	4.45m (14ft 7in)
Powerplant	one 970hp BMW 132K 9-cylinder radial	Weight	3730kg (8223lb) loaded
		Armament	two 20mm (0.78in) fixed forward-firing cannon in wing; one 7.92mm
Max speed	320km/h (199mph)		(0.31in) MG in starboard side of
Service ceiling	7000m (22,960ft)		forward fuselage and one 7.92mm
Max range	107km (665 miles)		(0.3in) in rear cockpit, plus external
Wing span	12.40m (50ft 9in)		bomb load of 100kg (220lb)
Length	11.00m (36ft)		

cation shows, it was heavily armed and had sufficient speed to engage the types of Allied maritime reconnaissance aircraft then in service.

For ease of stowage, the wings of the Arados were removed, being easily refitted as required by the servicing crew that accompanied the air detachment on the *Bismarck*. In the operational area, one aircraft was to be held at permanent readiness on the telescopic catapult running across the width of the vessel. Catapult take-offs, which could be made to both port and starboard, were assisted by compressed air, the aircraft being recovered by crane after completing its sortie.

FULL TRAINING

In April 1940, the first crew members came aboard, and on 23 June the *Bismarck* entered floating dry dock No. V–VI. Here, her three propellers and MES degaussing system, designed to protect her against magnetic mines, were installed over a three-week period. She left the dry dock on 14 July, and on 24 August, at 1230 hours, she was officially commissioned at the

Below: The *Bismarck*'s optical rangefinding equipment (seen here in fore- and background) enabled the distance to the target to be computed automatically. The unconventional ship's helm is in the centre.

Blohm & Voss Shipyard under Captain Ernst Lindemann, a blond, 45-year-old Rhinelander much respected by his colleagues. A chain-smoker who consumed enormous amounts of coffee, Lindemann was a gunnery expert with a thorough knowledge of engineering. Immediately after commissioning, the crew was organized into divisions and, while Bismarck continued fitting out, a full training programme was implemented. On the night of 25–26 August there was an air raid alert and Bismarck's AA gunners fired off 52 37mm (1.4in) and 400 20mm (0.78in) shells, which lit up the sky over Hamburg but produced no other visible result; the alarm was a consequence of RAF Bomber Command's first major attack on Germany, with 103 aircraft despatched to Berlin, Bremen, Cologne and Hamm. The raid on Berlin, which produced little damage, was in reprisal for an earlier incident in which Luftwaffe crews mistakenly bombed the London suburbs; the ordeal of the cities had begun.

Right: Close-up of *Prinz Eugen's* two 20.3cm (8in) gun turrets. The heavy cruiser and *Bismarck* would have made a strong fighting team, but the Germans never made use of them together.

Above: The Arado Ar 196 floatplane was carried by all the major German surface units by 1941. It was very agile and well armed, and operated in every theatre where the German Navy was engaged.

ACCEPTANCE TRIALS

On 15 September 1940, the *Bismarck* left Hamburg, passed along the Elbe and through the Kaiser Wilhelm canal, the 98-

The *Bismarck*

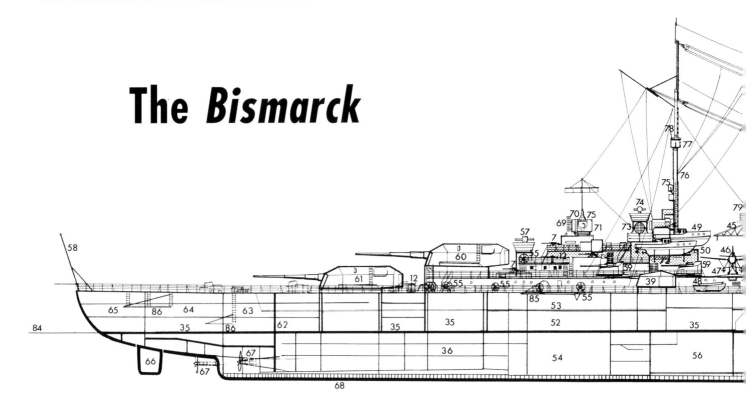

KEY BOX

1. Radar
2. Range finder
3. Armoured control tower
4. Admirals bridge
5. Searchlight
6. Day bridge
7. 37mm gun
8. Range finder
9. Radar
10. Gimbal-mounted AA gun
11. AA command post
12. 20mm gun
13. Armoured conning tower
14. Navigation room
15. Wing of bridge
16. Turret B: 380mm (15in)
17. Turret A: 390mm (15in)
18. Exhaust trunking
19. Gunsight telescope
20. Breech mortice
21. Shell tray
22. Toothed elevating gear
23. Training base on ball bearings
24. Elevating gear
25. Hydraulic pump
26. Machinery compartment
27. Auxiliary ammunition trunk
28. Barbette armour
29. Rammer
30. Crew quarters
31. Anchor gear

32. Battery deck
33. Stores
34. Forward armoured bulkhead
35. Armoured or lower deck
36. Honeycomb of bulkheads below armoured deck
37. Barbette B turret (main armament)
38. Machine stop
39. Barbette: secondary armament 150mm (5.9in) guns
40. Lifeboats
41. Catwalk
42. Motor lifeboats
43. Crane
44. Funnel uptakes
45. Boat crane
46. Arado 196 aircraft
47. Aircraft catapult gear
48. Lifeboat
49. Motor lifeboats
50. Hanger
51. Machine stop
52. Stores
53. Crew
54. Engine gear room
55. Water hose reels
56. Engine and boiler rooms
57. Anti-aircraft control
58. Aft ensign mast
59. Barbette secondary armament

60. Turret c: 380mm (15in) guns, main armament
61. Turret D: 380mm (15in) guns main armament
62. Aft armoured bulkhead
63. Winch room
64. Stores
65. Anchor gear
66. Rudder
67. Propeller shafts (3)
68. Ships double bottom
69. Radar
70. Aft superstructure
71. Armoured aft control positions
72. Boat stowage platform
73. Searchlight
74. AA control
75. Signalling lamp
76. Mainmast
77. Spotting positions
78. Rudder pointer
79. Remote control searchlight
80. Funnel
81. Searchlight with cover in positions
82. Fore mast
83. Radio aerials
84. Waterline
85. Gangways (2)
86. Boat sponsors

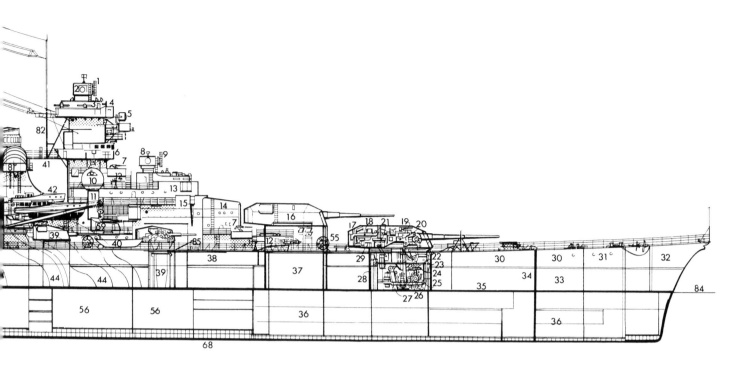

km (61-mile) waterway joining the North Sea and the Baltic. It anchored at Scheerhafen, Kiel, two days later. She remained there for ten days, aligning her batteries and embarking supplies, before proceeding to Gotenhafen (Gdynia) in the Bay of Danzig, which was to be her base while she conducted preliminary trials in the Baltic. During October and November she carried out numerous tasks connected with a warship's acceptance trials, adjusting compasses, testing degaussing gear, running machinery and speed trials, and working up to her top speed of 30 knots. On 5 December

she left the Baltic to complete her outfitting, returning through the Kiel Canal on 7–8 December, reaching Hamburg the next day. Back in the Blohm & Voss Shipyard and moored to the equipping pier, the *Bismarck* underwent final adjustments and had her last items of equipment installed, including the optical rangefinders and the full range of anti-aircraft

Below: The battleship *Bismarck* seen on the day of her completion, 24 August 1940. She began her acceptance trials in the Baltic three weeks later, returning to Hamburg to complete her outfitting in December.

Above: Ernst Lindemann, captain of the battleship *Bismarck*, pictured at the age of 45. A Rhinelander, Lindemann graduated top of his term as a naval cadet.

armament. The final touches were completed by the end of January 1941, and the *Bismarck* was ready to return to the Baltic for operational trials. She did not sail until 6 March, and in the meantime her sister ship, the *Tirpitz*, was commissioned on 25 February 1941.

CAMOUFLAGE

On 8 March, the *Bismarck*, having again passed through the Kiel Canal, embarked supplies at Scheerhafen in the course of the following week, while striped, dark-grey and white 'zig-zag' camouflage paint was applied to her hull. Superimposed on a grey band of paint, applied across the breadth of the deck near the bow, was a large swastika, necessary as an aircraft recognition marking. She also embarked two Ar 196 floatplanes.

Based once more on Gotenhafen, *Bismarck* began her final series of exercises in the Baltic on 18 March. While these were in progress, she was joined by the new 14,225-tonne (14,000-ton) heavy cruiser *Prinz Eugen*, whose captain, Helmuth Brinkmann from Lübeck, had been a classmate of Lindemann

at Naval College. In her own right, the *Prinz Eugen* was a formidable ship, as a look at her statistics reveals.

BATTLE SQUADRON

On 2 April 1941, the German Naval Staff issued preparatory orders for the deployment of *Bismarck* to the Atlantic. In the next new moon period at the end of the month the *Bismarck*, the *Prinz Eugen* and the battlecruiser *Gneisenau*, which was in Brest together with the Scharnhorst, were to rendezvous in the Atlantic for a combined attack on Allied shipping. *Scharnhorst* would be unable to join them because her boilers were being repaired. Yet even without her, it was a formidable battle squadron that was preparing to put to sea. Had it done so, the results might have been disastrous for Britain, for *Bismarck* was capable of engaging escorting warships while her two consorts attacked the convoys themselves. The carnage would have been terrible and the British had already had a taste of the destruction that could be meted out by major German surface units. However, events were to intervene, events that were the result of a series of engagements beginning some months previously.

On 22 January 1941, the *Scharnhorst* and the *Gneisenau* left Kiel and broke out into the North Sea, heading for the commerce routes of the North Atlantic. They were sighted in

Below: *Bismarck* seen near Kiel during the final phase of her trials. The Germans cancelled six even larger battleships in 1940, in the belief that the war was won and that they were not needed.

Above: With the date for Operation Rhine Exercise approaching, the *Bismarck*'s crew apply camouflage paint to the mighty battleship's hull. Photograph taken in Kiel, March 1941.

passage on the following day, and the British Home Fleet, commanded by Admiral Sir John Tovey, set out to intercept them south of Iceland. Patrolling cruisers sighted them as they tried to break through, but contact was broken and the German warships withdrew into the Arctic for replenishment. On the night of 3–4 February, they passed through the Denmark Strait undetected.

On 8 February, in the North Atlantic, they sighted the British convoy HX106 east of Newfoundland, but the Fleet Commander, Admiral Günther Lütjens, thought it prudent not to attack as the merchantmen were escorted by the battleship HMS *Ramillies*. On 22 February, however, still about 925km (500nm) east of Newfoundland, they fell upon a westbound convoy that had dispersed and sunk five ships totalling 26,198 tonnes (25,784 tons).

On Saturday 15 March 1941, the two warships were operating in the central North Atlantic when they encountered the scattered ships of another dispersed convoy. The result was a massacre. The *Gneisenau* sank seven freighters totalling 27,122 tonnes (26,693 tons) and captured three tankers of 20,462 tonnes (20,139 tons), while the *Scharnhorst* sank six ships totalling 35,562 tonnes (35,080 tons). The *Gneisenau* had a narrow escape; as she was picking up survivors from her last victim, she was surprised by the battleship HMS *Rodney*, whose captain, alerted by a

distress call, had detached his ship from convoy XH114 and rushed to the scene. Captain Fein, making good use of the *Gneisenau*'s superior speed and manoeuvrability, managed to avoid an engagement with his heavier-armed opponent, and got away.

The British Admiralty immediately launched a major operation to trap the German warships, sending the battleships HMS *Rodney* and *King George V* north, to join a third battleship, *Nelson*, a cruiser and two destroyers in covering the Iceland passages. Meanwhile, Force H, with the battlecruiser *Renown*, the aircraft carrier *Ark Royal*, the cruiser *Sheffield* and some destroyers, set out from Gibraltar to cover the approaches to the French Atlantic ports, and on 20 March a Swordfish reconnaissance aircraft from the carrier sighted the tankers captured by the *Gneisenau*. With Force H coming up fast, the prize crews were forced to scuttle two of the vessels, but the third managed to evade the British warships and reached the Gironde eastuary. The two German battlecruisers were also sighted by a Swordfish later in the day, but the aircraft had radio trouble and by the time its sighting report was transmitted the warships had slipped away. On 22 March they

31

were met by the torpedo boats *Iltis* and *Jaguar* and some minesweepers and escorted into Brest. Their sortie had cost the Allies 22 ships totalling 117,478 tonnes (115,622 tons).

Photographic reconnaissance did not detect the presence of the German warships at Brest until 28 March, and as soon as he learned of it Winston Churchill issued a directive that the battlecruisers were to become a primary target for RAF Bomber Command. The air offensive against them began on the night of 30-31 March, when 109 aircraft were despatched to attack Brest harbour without result. There was a further abortive attack on 4-5 April by 54 aircraft; their bombs caused considerable damage to the town and one fell in the dry dock alongside the *Gneisenau* without exploding. Her captain thought it advisable to move the ship to the outer harbour, where she would be safer if the bomb detonated while it was being disarmed.

She was located by a photo-reconnaissance Spitfire, and a strike by Coastal Command aircraft was arranged. The sortie was flown at dawn on 6 April 1941 by six Bristol Beauforts of No. 22 Squadron from St Eval, in Cornwall, but only one succeeded in locating the target in bad visibility. Its pilot, Flying Officer Kenneth Campbell, made his torpedo run at mast height through intense flak put up by more than 250 guns around the anchorage, as well as by three flak ships and the *Gneisenau*'s own armament. The Beaufort was shot down with the loss of all its crew, but not before Campbell had released his torpedo at a range of 457m (500 yards). The torpedo exploded on the *Gneisenau*'s stern below the waterline, putting the cruiser out of action for months. For

his gallant action, Campbell was posthumously awarded the Victoria Cross. The other members of his crew were Sergeants J.P. Scott, W. Mullis and R.W. Hillman. It was one of the most gallant, and in retrospect the most important, deeds of the war.

The German Navy Commander-in-Chief, Admiral Raeder, was now faced with a dilemma. He could postpone the planned attack until the *Bismarck*'s sister ship, the *Tirpitz*, was ready to join her; but she was only just about to begin her trials, and the longer the mission was delayed, the less chance there would be of the ships breaking out into the Atlantic unseen, for the northern nights would soon be short. What probably tilted the scales in favour of an immediate sortie was the fact that German forces had just invaded Greece, and any diversion that might prevent reinforcements from reaching the British Mediterranean Fleet would be valuable.

On 8 April 1941, Fleet Commander Admiral Günther Lütjens, fresh from his Atlantic raiding experiences with the battlecruisers, flew to Paris to confer with Admiral Karl Dönitz about co-operation between *Bismarck* and U-boats. Then, on 24 April, came a further setback; the *Prinz Eugen* was damaged by a magnetic mine, and a fortnight was needed to make repairs. Once again, Raeder was forced to consider postponement, but despite the fact that Lütjens was in favour of it – at least until the *Scharnhorst* or the *Tirpitz* was ready – he decid-

Below: Although the British classed the *Gneisenau* and her sister ship *Scharnhorst* as battlecruisers, the Germans always referred to them as battleships, which was probably a much more accurate description.

Lindemann's steward, who had been a waiter in Lindemann's favourite Hamburg restaurant. He had not liked the idea of military service, but had been happy to go to sea in a warship that was so large, powerful and safe.

As the day of *Bismarck*'s departure approached, the small fleet of escort vessels that would accompany her on the first leg of her voyage began to assemble. Foremost among them were three of Germany's latest destroyers: Z-10 *Hans Lody*, commanded by Fregattenkapitän Werner Pfeiffer, which also carried the officer commanding the 6th Destroyer Flotilla, Fregattenkapitän Alfred Schulze-Hinrichs; Z-16 *Friedrich Eckoldt*, under Fregattenkapitän Alfred Schemmel; and Z-23, under Fregattenkapitän Friedrich Böhme. Clearing a path ahead of the warships would be the 5th Minesweeping Flotilla, commanded by Korvettenkapitän Rudolf Lell, while three small flak ships guarded their flanks. Already at sea, in the *Bismarck*'s operational area, were 16 U-boats deployed to intercept any British warships; while a fleet of 20 tankers, supply vessels and weather ships was strung out along the warships' route, from the Arctic to mid-Atlantic.

Within a month, most of them, like the *Bismarck*, would be at the bottom of the sea.

ed to go ahead with the sortie at the earliest opportunity. At the beginning of May, Lütjens flew to Gotenhafen and embarked on the *Bismarck* with the officers of his staff. The operation was allocated a codename, Rheinubung (Rhine Exercise); the starting date was to be 18 May.

On 5 May, Adolf Hitler paid a visit to Gotenhafen, accompanied by, among others, General Keitel, Chief of the General Staff, and Captain von Puttkamer, Hitler's naval aide. Hitler spent four hours on board *Bismarck*, listening in fascination, according to some accounts, to the technical explanations that were handed out to him. He then moved on to the *Tirpitz*, which was at Gotenhafen for trials, having been completed a few weeks earlier. One of the men accompanying him, Walther Hewel (Foreign Minister Joachim von Ribbentrop's liaison officer at Hitler's HQ), wrote in his diary that night: 'Visit unbelievably impressive. Concentration of force and the highest technical development.'

One of the men who waited on Hitler's entourage during their visit to the *Bismarck* was Captain Ernst

Right: The *Bismarck* in line astern, photographed from the *Prinz Eugen* during trials in the Baltic; the two warships were exercising together prior to their sortie.

CHAPTER 3

Bismarck: The Fatal Voyage

Bismarck and *Prinz Eugen* was the most powerful warship duo afloat. They were to have been joined by the battlecruisers *Scharnhorst* and *Gneisenau*.

On the morning of Sunday, 18 May, Admiral Lütjens held a final conference in his cabin, attended by his staff officers and the captains of the two warships. His operational brief came from Admiral Carls of Naval Group Command North in Wilhelmshaven, who had shore authority over the sortie until the ships crossed the line between southern Greenland and the Hebrides, when it was to come under the control of Group Command West in Paris. Carls recommended sailing direct to Korsfjord near Bergen and remaining there for a day while the *Prinz Eugen*, whose radius of action was limited, replenished her tanks. The ships were then to sail direct for the Atlantic through the Iceland-Faeroes gap. Lütjens' intention, however, was to bypass Korsfjord and proceed directly to the Arctic Ocean, refuel from the tanker Weissenburg near Jan Mayen Island, and then make a high-speed dash for the Atlantic through the Denmark Straits. After the conference, Lütjens went over to the *Prinz Eugen* to carry out an inspection.

DIRE CONSEQUENCES

The two warships left harbour shortly after 1100 hours and dropped anchor in the Roads, and at 1130 hours the crews of both warships were told that Rheinübung was about to begin. In the afternoon, the *Bismarck* and the *Prinz Eugen* carried out exercises with the Tirpitz off the coast, the *Prinz Eugen* testing her degaussing equipment, dropping anchor again in the Roads early in the afternoon. The next few hours were spent in taking on fuel oil. Earlier, several Polish labourers had been killed by toxic fumes while cleaning the oil tanks, and this mishap may have had something to do with the decision not to oil to full capacity, for fear of more dangerous fumes being vented. It was a decision that would have dire consequences. At about 0200 hours on Monday 19 May 1941, both warships weighed anchor and proceeded westwards independently. At 1100 hours, they made rendezvous

Left: Radiating power, the *Bismarck* is pictured at anchor in Hamburg after her acceptance trials. These revealed a number of snags, all of which were relatively easy to put right.

off Arkona, the northernmost cape of Prussia, and continued with their escort of minesweepers and destroyers. All that day, and through the night, the squadron sailed in formation westward and northward, the escorts followed by Bismarck and Prinz Eugen. Skirting the eastern edge of Kiel Bay, the ships passed through the Great Belt, the seaway that divides the two parts of Denmark, at about 0200 hours on Tuesday morning.

MOVEMENT BETRAYED

For security reasons, Group North had placed an embargo on all shipping movements in the area during the squadron's passage into the North Sea, but this did not affect vessels flying a flag of neutrality. At 1300 hours on 20 May, the force was reported in the Kattegat by the Swedish cruiser Gotland, which accompanied the German ships at a discreet distance for several hours until they turned away to port off Marstrand, making for the Skaggerak and a landfall at Kristiansand, in southern Norway. Gotland sent a routine signal to Stockholm, and on board the Bismarck Admiral Lütjens contacted Group North, expressing the belief that the movement of his squadron had been betrayed. His suspicions were no doubt heightened when, between 1400 and 1800 hours on the 20th, numerous steamers, fishing boats and other small craft were sighted.

In fact, a signal concerning Bismarck's whereabouts was already on its way to London via one Captain Henry Denham, RN, a British agent in Stockholm, who had received the intelligence from contacts in the Swedish secret service. Denham's coded telegram to the British Admiralty was brief and to the point: 'Kattegat today 20th May. At 1500 two large warships, escorted by three destroyers, five escort vessels,

Left: Admiral Günther Lütjens, the Fleet Commander, and members of his staff inspecting the crew of the battleship Bismarck prior to her departure on her fateful voyage in May 1941.

Above: The Focke-Wulf Fw 200 Kondor maritime patrol aircraft, operating from bases in Norway, made wide-ranging flights into the Arctic to survey the route that would be taken by Bismarck and Prinz Eugen.

ten or twelve aircraft, passed Marstrand course north-west. 2058/20.'

In the early evening, several Norwegians were walking on the shore near Kristiansand when they sighted a group of warships steaming towards the fjords at high speed. Two were large, camouflaged vessels; small ships preceded them, and twin-engined Messerschmitt 110 fighters cruised overhead. One of the group, Viggo Axelssen, was a member of the Norwegian Resistance, and his observation of the enemy force's northward movement swiftly followed Denham's report, reaching the British Admiralty in the early hours of 21 May.

There had already been other indications that the German warships were about to make a sortie. Naval intelligence had established that the Bismarck and the Prinz Eugen had completed their working-up period, and an agent in Germany had reported that new charts had just been delivered to the Bismarck. From agents in France came the news that the Germans were preparing moorings for large vessels at Brest. German air reconnaissance of the British naval base at Scapa Flow had been stepped up, and Focke-Wulf Kondor maritime patrol aircraft had been sighted over the Denmark Strait, between Greenland and Iceland, and between Greenland and Jan Mayen Island. These were undoubtedly weather reconnaissance flights, and they could only mean that German naval forces were about to atempt a breakout into the Atlantic. Admiral Sir John Tovey, the Commander-in-Chief Home Fleet, at once strengthened surveillance of the northern passages into the Atlantic, ordering the battleship Prince of Wales, the battlecruiser Hood and six destroyers to sail from Scapa Flow under Vice-Admiral Lancelot Holland, flying his flag in the Hood. Meanwhile, reconnaissance aircraft were despatched to search for the enemy warships.

ZIG-ZAG PATTERN

At 0630 hours on Wednesday 21 May, the B-Dienst (wireless intelligence service) office on the *Prinz Eugen* decoded some British signals traffic indicating that reconnaissance aircraft had been despatched to hunt for the German naval force. Throughout the night of 20–21 May, the force steamed northwards up the Norwegian coast, following a zigzag pattern to avoid British submarines. At 0900 hours on 21 May, Lütjens ordered the task force to enter the Norwegian fjords instead of making for the Atlantic with all speed. The *Bismarck* entered Korsfjord and then Grimstad fjord, just south of Bergen, while the *Prinz Eugen* went into Kalvanes Bay, to the north-west; the destroyer escorts went to Bergen. Lütjens signalled the cruiser to take on oil from the tanker *Wollin* and to be ready to sail in the evening. Meanwhile, four merchant ships were ordered alongside each of the big warships, one on each beam and quarter, as anti-torpedo protection for the engine rooms, propellers and rudders.

That same afternoon, the *Bismarck* and her consort were photographed by a Photographic Reconnaissance Unit Spitfire, one of two sent out to look for the ships. The Spitfire pilot, Fg Off Michael Suckling, landed at Wick in north-east Scotland, where his film was developed; he then made a high-speed dash south with the precious prints, but was forced to make an emergency landing near his home town of Nottingham because of dense cloud. Rousing a friend who was a garage proprietor, Suckling continued his journey in the latter's car, driving through the blackout at dangerous speeds. Eventually, at 0100 hours on 22 May, unshaven and still wearing his flying kit, he arrived at the Air Ministry in London, where he handed over the package of photographs to Air Chief Marshal Sir Frederick Bowhill, AOC-in-C Coastal Command.

Above: The British King George V class battleship *Prince of Wales* at anchor. Launched in May 1939, she was not yet fully completed when the *Bismarck* and *Prinz Eugen* made their breakout into the Atlantic.

SLIPPED AWAY

Less than two hours after Suckling had walked into Bowhill's office, aircraft of Coastal Command were on their way to attack the German warships, but their operations were frustrated by bad weather. Shortly before nightfall on the 22nd, a Martin Maryland reconnaissance aircraft of No. 771 Naval Air Squadron from Hatston in the Orkneys penetrated Korsfjord, but its crew, Lt N.E. Goddard RNVR (pilot) and Commander G.A. Rotherham (observer) returned with the news that the *Bismarck* and the *Prinz Eugen* were gone. In fact, they had already slipped away at 2200 hours the previous evening, continuing on a northerly heading in the company of their three destroyer escorts.

At 2245 hours, Admiral Tovey left Scapa Flow with the main body of the Home Fleet, heading for Icelandic waters to reinforce the heavy cruisers HMS *Norfolk* and *Suffolk*, which were patrolling the Denmark Strait. Three more cruisers were guarding Lütjens' alternative breakout route, between Iceland and the Faeroes. First to arrive were the Home Fleet's two fastest ships, HMS *Prince of Wales* and the *Hood*, which had set out in advance of the main force; behind them came Tovey's Fleet Flagship, the new battleship *King George V*, the aircraft carrier *Victorious*, four cruisers and six destroyers. The carrier was not yet fully worked up, and her air group comprised only nine Fairey Swordfish torpedo/reconnaissance aircraft and six

Right: The *Prinz Eugen* survived the war, seeing service in the Baltic during the final months. Handed over to the Americans, she also survived the atomic bomb tests at Bikini Atoll in 1946, but was sunk in 1947.

HMS *Hood*

Fairey Fulmar fighters. She had been earmarked to escort Convoy WS.8B, bound for the Middle East with troops, but had been released on Admiralty orders to take part in the hunt for the *Bismarck*. So had the battlecruiser *Repulse*, which also sailed north accompanied by three destroyers withdrawn from the Western Approaches.

SINISTER SHAPE

At 1922 hours on 23 May, Able Seaman Newall, a young look-out on the cruiser *Suffolk* was keeping watch on the Denmark Strait, sweeping the sea with his powerful binoculars. The cruiser was patrolling the ice shelf, and although the visibility towards Greenland was good, there was thick mist in the direction of Iceland, with occasional flurries of snow. It was from that direction that Newall now saw a sinister dark shape emerging from the murk, followed by another, and he reported his sighting. Captain Robert Ellis ordered hard-a-port and full speed ahead, making for the safety of a fog bank as the battleship bore down on the *Suffolk* less than 11km (7 miles) away. He waited for the *Bismarck*'s first salvo; it never came. The Suffolk ran on through the fog, her radar keeping track of the enemy ships

Above: Launched in August 1918, the battlecruiser HMS *Hood* was the pride of the Royal Navy in the years between the two world wars. Her fatal flaw was that her designers sacrificed armour for speed.

as they passed her. Ellis held his course for 21km (13 miles), then emerged from the fog and took up station astern of the *Prinz Eugen*. Eventually, about an hour after AB Newall's first sighting, Suffolk was joined by HMS *Norfolk*, which had been coming up fast, alerted by her sister ship's signals. She emerged from the fog to find the *Bismarck* only six miles ahead, coming straight at her. The cruiser's skipper was Captain Alfred Phillips, and she was flying the flag of Rear-Admiral W.F. Wake-Walker, commanding the 1st Cruiser Squadron. Phillips at once ordered a turn to starboard, and at that moment the *Bismarck* opened fire.

The *Norfolk* came under enemy fire at a range of 11,880m (13,000 yards) and was straddled by three 38cm (15in) salvoes before retiring under cover of smoke, miraculously

Right: HMS *Hood* in action during a pre-war fleet exercise, pictured from the battlecruiser HMS *Repulse*. The latter, together with the *Prince of Wales*, would be sunk by Japanese air attack in December 1941.

HMS *HOOD* DATA AT A GLANCE			
Displacement	41,000t (45,200t full load)		bulkheads 102–127mm (4–5in) decks
Dimensions	860ft 7in x 105ft x 31ft 6in		26-76mm (1–3in)
	(262.3m x 32m x 9.6m)	**Armament**	4 x 380mm (15in); 12 x 140mm
Machinery	4 screws, Brown-Curtis geared		(5.5in); 4 x 102mm (4in); 8 x 102mm
	turbines, 24 Yarrow boilers;144,000hp		AA: 4 x 533mm (21in) TT
Max speed	32 knots	**Complement**	1477
Endurance	6300nm (11,674km) at 12 knots	**Aircraft**	2
Armour	belt and barbettes 127–305mm (5–	**Launched**	1918
	12in); turrets 280-380mm (11–15in);		

undamaged, to radio her enemy sighting report to Admiral Tovey, whose main fleet was still some 1110km (600nm) to the south-west. The two cruisers continued to shadow Lütjens' ships at high speed throughout the night, the *Suffolk* maintaining contact with her Type 284 radar.

The *Prince of Wales* and the *Hood*, meanwhile, were coming up quickly; Vice-Admiral Holland's ships had been about 408km (220nm) away at the time of the first sighting report, and Holland was anticipating a night action. His plan was to concentrate the fire of his heavy ships on the *Bismarck*, leaving Wake-Walker's cruisers to deal with the *Prinz Eugen*. What he did not know was that the *Bismarck* was no longer in the lead; the blast from her guns had put her own forward radar out of action, so Lütjens had ordered the *Prinz Eugen* to change position.

INTERCEPTION COURSE

As his heavy ships approached, Vice-Admiral Holland, conscious of the need for surprise, imposed strict radio and radar silence, relying on *Suffolk*'s reports to keep him informed of the enemy's position. Soon after midnight, however, *Suffolk* lost contact, and did not regain it until 0247 hours. In the meantime, Holland had turned his ships south to await full daylight, but when information once again began to come through from the *Suffolk* he increased speed to 28 knots and turned on an interception course. It was now 0340 hours, and visibility was 19km (12 miles).

At 0537 hours, the opposing forces sighted each other at a range of 31km (17nm), and opened fire at 0553 hours. Both German ships concentrated their fire on the *Hood* and, thanks to their stereoscopic rangefinders, straddled her

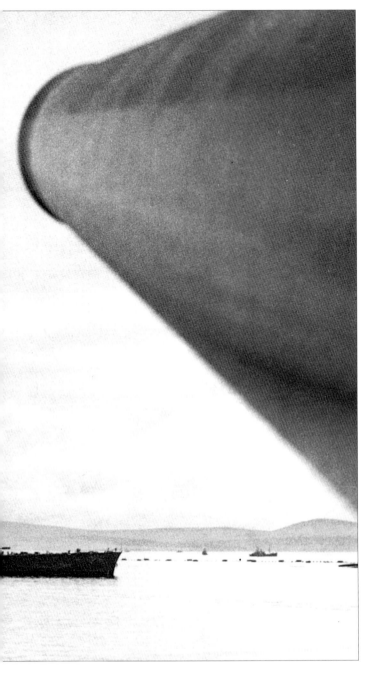

Left: Framed by the big guns of another battleship, HMS *Hood* lies peacefully at anchor in Scapa Flow. In the inter-war years, no other ship did as much to 'show the flag' for Britain around the world.

immediately; the *Bismarck*'s second and third salvoes struck the battlecruiser amidships, and those from the *Prinz Eugen* started a fire among her ready-to-use AA ammunition.

At 0600 hours, as the British warships were altering course in order to bring all their guns to bear, the *Hood* was hit again by a salvo that pierced her lightly armoured decks and detonated in her aft magazines. She blew up with a tremendous explosion and disappeared with a speed that stunned all who witnessed the event. Only three of her crew of 1419 officers and ratings survived. According to modern theories, supported by underwater photography of the Hood's widely scattered wreckage, the *Bismarck*'s shell ignited the 102 tonnes (100 tons) of cordite in the aft magazines, causing a massive firestorm that burned its way through the ship's interior like a huge blowlamp flame. When the conflagration reached the engine room vents, it shot upwards, but flames also continued forward through the machinery spaces, venting upwards around the bridge and igniting the forward magazines.

HEAVY FIRE

As the *Prince of Wales* altered course sharply to avoid the wreckage, she herself came under heavy fire. Within moments, she sustained hits by four 38cm (15in) and three 20cm (8in) shells. One of these passed through the bridge, exploding as it went, and killed or wounded everyone there except the chief yeoman of signals and the captain, J.C. Leach, who ordered the battleship to turn away under cover of smoke. Another shell hit the superstructure supporting the gun directors that controlled the forward secondary armament of 14cm (5.5in) guns and put them out of action. A third smashed the wings of the ship's spotter aircraft, which was on the point of being catapulted off; the crew scrambled clear and the dangerous, fuel-laden wreck was tipped over the side. Yet another shell penetrated the hull

FAIREY SWORDFISH DATA AT A GLANCE			
Type	torpedo/ASW/reconnaissance aircraft	**Wing area**	56.39sq m (607.0ft²)
		Length	10.87m (35ft 8in)
Crew	3	**Height**	3.76m (12ft 4in)
Powerplant	one 820hp Bristol Pegasus XXX radial engine	**Weights**	empty 2132kg (4700lb); max t/o 3406kg (7510lb)
Max speed	222km/h (138mph)	**Armament**	one fixed forward-firing 7.7mm
Initial climb rate	372m (1220ft) per minute		(0.303in) machine gun and one
Service ceiling	5867m (19250ft)		trainable 7.7mm (0.303in) gun in rear
Max range	879km (546 miles)		cockpit, plus an offensive load of one
Wing span	12.97m (45ft 6in)		457mm (18in) torpedo

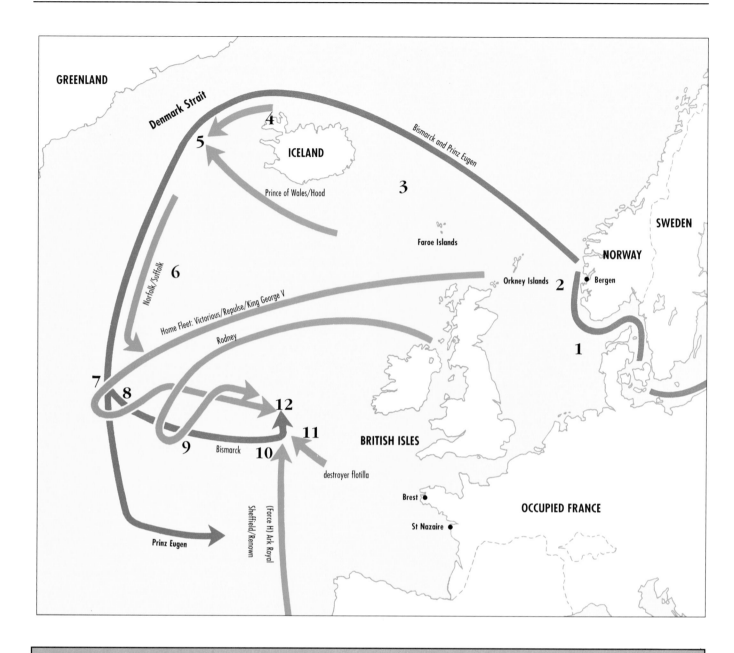

THE HUNT FOR THE *BISMARCK*

1. The *Bismarck* and the *Prinz Eugen* break out into the North Sea, 20 May 1941; Norwegian agents report their movement to the British Admiralty
2. The *Bismarck* and the *Prinz Eugen* detected at Bergen by air reconnaissance, but succeed in escaping, 22 May 1941
3. British cruisers *Arethusa*, *Birmingham* and *Manchester* patrol Iceland–Faroes passage
4. The *Bismarck* and the *Prinz Eugen* detected and shadowed by cruisers *Suffolk* and *Norfolk* in Denmark Strait, 23 May 1941
5. The *Bismarck* and the *Prinz Eugen* engaged by battle-cruiser *Hood* and battleship *Prince of Wales* (Battle of the Denmark Strait). *Hood* sunk, *Prince of Wales* and *Bismarck* damaged, 24 May 1941

6. British cruisers continue to shadow enemy warships until contact lost
7. Warships of the Home Fleet, including aircraft carrier *Victorious*, sail to intercept enemy warships
8. The *Prince Eugen* detached on lone raiding sortie; German Fleet Commander decides to make for Brest with the *Bismarck*, 24 May 1941
9. The *Bismarck* unsuccessfully attacked by Swordfish torpedo-bombers from HMS *Victorious*, 25 May 1941
10. The *Bismarck* sighted by Catalina flying boat of No. 209 Squadron, RAF Coastal Command, 26 May 1941
11. *Ark Royal* launches a successful torpedo attack on the *Bismarck*. One torpedo hit jams the battleship's rudders
12. The *Bismarck* attacked by destroyers during the night, 27 May 1941

deep under water, passing through several bulkheads and coming to rest without exploding near the diesel dynamo room. It was only discovered after the battleship returned to harbour. Two of the 20.3cm (8in) shells had pierced the ship's side aft, on the waterline, allowing 500 tons of water to pour in. The third entered one of the 13.3cm (5.25in) shell handling rooms, bounced round the confined space like a streak of lightning, then expended its energy and fell to the floor, also without exploding. By some miracle, no one was hurt.

The *Prince of Wales* was so newly completed that she had not yet finished working-up; the contractors were still working on her 35.5cm (14in) turrets when she sailed, and she was therefore not fully battleworthy, a fact of which Captain Leach was obviously conscious. The additional damage had made her even more vulnerable, and Leach's intention now was to use his damaged ship to assist Wake-Walker's cuisers in maintaining contact with the enemy until Admiral Tovey's main force could reach the scene.

THREE HITS

What Leach had no means of knowing was that his gunners had obtained three hits on the *Bismarck*, causing two of her fuel tanks to leak oil and contaminating others. As a result, Lütjens had decided to abandon the sortie and steer southwest for St Nazaire, the only port on the Atlantic coast of France with a dry dock large enough to accommodate his flagship while repairs were carried out.

Tovey's ships were still 612km (330nm) to the south-east and could not expect to make contact until 0700 hours on 25 May at the earliest. However, other ships were also heading for the scene. Admiral Somerville's Force H had been ordered north from Gibraltar by the Admiralty to intercept the German squadron, and the battleships *Rodney*, *Revenge*

Above: The battleship *Bismarck* firing a salvo from her main armament. The photo was taken in daylight; the dark effect is caused by the vivid flash of the warship's guns.

and *Ramillies* and the cruiser *Edinburgh* were also released from escort duties to take part in the chase. The main concern now was to reduce the *Bismarck*'s speed, giving the hunters a chance to close in for the kill, and at 1440 hours on 24 May, Admiral Tovey ordered the carrier *Victorious* to race ahead to a flying-off point 185km (100nm) from the enemy ships and launch a Swordfish strike against them.

At 2210 hours, *Victorious* flew off nine Swordfish of No. 825 Squadron, led by Lt Cdr Eugene Esmonde. Flying through rain and sleet, they obtained radar contact with the enemy at 2337 hours and briefly sighted the *Bismarck*, only to lose her again. Twenty minutes later, the shadowing British cruisers redirected the Swordfish on to their target and they made their attack through heavy defensive fire. One torpedo hit the *Bismarck* amidships without causing significant damage; the other eight missed. All the attacking Swordfish recovered safely to the carrier, although two reconnaissance Fulmars out of six despatched failed to return. The returning crews reported no sign of the *Prinz Eugen*, which had in fact been detached by Admiral Lütjens to continue on her way alone.

THE FAIREY SWORDFISH

The Fairey Swordfish, known universally as the 'Stringbag', appeared to be an anachronism from the moment of its conception; a slow, lumbering biplane that seemed to have no place in the increasingly streamlined world of 1930s aviation. Yet the design of the Swordfish was exactly right for the principal tasks it had to perform, and its rugged structure made it ideal for aircraft carrier operations. It was to serve

Above: Shells from the battlecruiser _Hood_ drop short of the _Prinz Eugen_. When the Battle of the Denmark Strait began, the heavy cruiser was in the lead, and was mistaken for the _Bismarck_.

craft was placed in April 1935, the aircraft entering service with No. 825 Squadron of the Fleet Air Arm in July 1936. Production aircraft were built to Specification S.38/34, featuring a slightly swept-back upper wing, all-metal construction with a fabric covering, and a Bristol Pegasus IIIM.3 engine. The Swordfish I was designed to carry a 730kg (1610lb) torpedo under the fuselage, but as an alternative load it could carry a 680kg (1500lb) mine in the same position, or an equivalent weight of bombs distributed under the fuselage and lower wings.

By the outbreak of World War II, 689 Swordfish had been delivered or were on order. Thirteen squadrons were equipped with the type, and a further 12 were formed during the war years. Early war roles for the Swordfish included fleet escort and convoy protection, the first offensive missions being flown during the Norwegian campaign, April–June 1940. It was in the Mediterranean Theatre that the Swordfish really proved its worth. On 3–4 July, during the tragic but necessary attack on the French fleet at Mers-el-Kebir, Swordfish from HMS _Ark Royal_ disabled the French flagship _Dunkerque_. The following day, shore-based Swordfish from Egypt attacked Axis shipping in Tobruk harbour, sinking one Italian destroyer and damaging another, and also sinking a large freighter and damaging the troopship _Liguria_.

In the months that followed, Swordfish inflicted considerable damage on Italian shipping, culminating in the spectacular night attack on the Italian fleet at Taranto on 11

with great distinction throughout World War II, from the North Atlantic to the Indian Ocean, and in so doing performed feats of arms that became legendary.

The Swordfish was derived from the private-venture Fairey TSR 1, the prototype of which was lost in an accident in September 1933. Undeterred, the Fairey Aviation Company's design team followed up with a slightly larger development, the TSR II (Torpedo-Spotter-Reconnaissance II). The prototype, K4190, flew for the first time on 17 April 1934 and a contract for 86 production Swordfish Mk I air-

Below: 24 May 1941. _Bismarck_ engaging HMS _Hood_ shortly before the British ship's eventual sinking. This photograph was taken from the _Prinz Eugen_.

Above: An artist's impression of Fairey Swordfish torpedo bombers launching the fatal attack on the *Bismarck*. A torpedo hit jammed the battleship's rudders 15 degrees to port, leaving her unable to manoeuvre.

November 1940 by 21 Swordfish of Nos 815 and 819 Squadrons from HMS *Illustrious*. Twelve of the Swordfish were armed with torpedoes; the others carried flares for target illumination, and bombs for use against oil installations on shore. The attack was brilliantly successful. The Italian battleship *Conte di Cavour* was so badly damaged that she took no further part in hostilities; her sister ship, the *Caio Duilio*, had to be beached and was out of action for six months; while the *Littorio* was disabled for four months. At one stroke, the Italian battle fleet had been reduced from six to three capital ships at a crucial period of the Mediterranean war, and for the loss of only two Swordfish. It was the first real demonstration of the aircraft carrier as a means of exercising flexible, mobile sea power, and the lesson was not lost on the Japanese Admiral Isoroku Yamamoto, whose carrier aircraft attacked Pearl Harbor just over a year later.

Other notable Swordfish actions, before that against the *Bismarck*, included the Battle of Cape Matapan in March 1941.

At 0300 hours on 25 May, Lütjens altered course to the south-east, and at this critical juncture the shadowing cruisers, which had been following at extreme radar range, lost contact. The problems facing *Bismarck*'s pursuers were compounded after the Admiralty transmitted some bearings that, through a combination of errors, led Admiral Tovey to believe the battleship to be heading north-east, into the Atlantic. As a result, Tovey's flagship, *King George V*, and many other pursuing vessels followed this false trail throughout most of the day, until, at about 1800 hours, he decided that the *Bismarck* was probably heading for Brest and changed course accordingly. A signal received at 1924 hours indicated that the Admiralty also thought that this was the case. Indeed, the Admiralty, much earlier in the day, had already instructed Admiral Somerville's Force H to position itself on a line from which its ships and aircraft could intercept the *Bismarck* should she head for the Bay of Biscay. It turned out to be a fortuitous move.

STRICT SECRET

Although Tovey's warships had lost valuable ground during their false quest to the north-east, the net around the

Above: Although slow and obsolescent, the Fairey Swordfish torpedo bomber achieved some remarkable results in World War II, not least of which was the disabling of the Italian Fleet at Taranto in 1940.

Bismarck was gradually closing. It was now that the experience and tactical awareness of one man came into play. Air Chief Marshal Bowhill, who had served in the Royal Navy as a young man, persuaded his colleagues in the Admiralty that Admiral Lütjens would not steer directly for Brest, but would instead make his landfall at Cape Finisterre. Coastal Command's search aircraft were accordingly instructed to patrol well to the south, and at 1030 hours on the 26th, the *Bismarck* was sighted nearly 1297km (700nm) west of Brest by a Catalina of No. 209 Squadron from Castle Archdale (Lough Erne) in Northern Ireland. The aircraft's captain was Flying Officer Dennis Briggs, but the warship was actually

Below: Her slender outline easily distinguishable from the blunt silhouettes of supply vessels, *Bismarck* is photographed in Grimstadfjord by Plt Off Suckling's PRU Spitfire. The hunt was on.

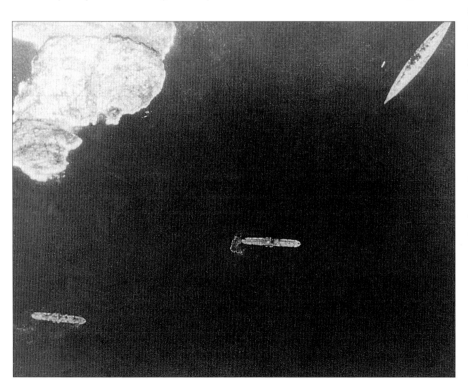

sighted by his co-pilot, US Navy Ensign Leonard B. Smith, one of several US Navy pilots gaining operational experience with Coastal Command. As the United States was still neutral, Smith's presence on the aircraft was kept a strict secret.

Soon after the Catalina crew sighted the *Bismarck*, contact was also made by two Swordfish reconnaissance aircraft from the *Ark Royal*, Force H's aircraft carrier. Admiral Somerville duly sent the cruiser *Sheffield* to shadow the battleship with her Type 79Y radar and, when the opportunity arose, to direct a strike by the carrier's Swordfish torpedo-bombers. Fourteen of the latter were flown off at 1450 hours in conditions of high winds, driving rain and rough seas, and some time later their radar revealed a target that their crews assumed was the *Bismarck*. In fact, it was the *Sheffield*, whose presence in the area had not been signalled to *Ark Royal*. The Swordfish came down through low cloud and attacked from different directions; several of them released their torpedoes before the mistake was recognized, but a fortunate combination of effective evasive manoeuvring by the cruiser and faulty magnetic pistols fitted to the torpedoes meant that no damage was caused.

CO-ORDINATED ATTACK

This first (and somewhat penitent) strike force returned to the carrier, which at 1910 hours launched a second wave of fifteen Swordfish. The aircraft, led by Lt Cdr T.P. Coode, were directed to the target by the *Sheffield*, but in the prevailing weather conditions, coupled with fading light and heavy defensive fire, they had little chance of making a co-ordinated attack. Nevertheless, two torpedoes found their mark; one struck the *Bismarck*'s armoured belt and did

little damage, but the other struck her extreme stern, damaging her propellers and jamming her rudders 15 degrees to port. At 2140 hours, Admiral Lütjens signalled Berlin: 'Ship no longer manoeuvrable. We fight to the last shell. Long live the Führer.'

Shortly afterwards, five destroyers, led by Captain Philip Vian in HMS *Cossack*, arrived on the scene, having been detached from convoy duty. They made contact with the *Bismarck* and shadowed her throughout the night, transmitting regular position reports and closing in to make a series of determined torpedo attacks, but these were disrupted by heavy and accurate radar-controlled gunfire. Whether any torpedoes hit their target or not is still a mystery; the destroyer crews maintained that they saw two explosions on the *Bismarck*, but the survivors of the battleship later stated that no hits were made. Whatever the truth, the *Bismarck* was seen to reduce speed, and her destruction was now inevitable.

NO ESCAPE

During the night, the battleships *King George V* and *Rodney* came within striking distance of their crippled enemy. However, Admiral Tovey, aware of the accuracy of her radar-directed gunnery, decided to wait until daylight before engaging her; she had no means of escaping him now. Yet *King George V* herself, and the carrier *Ark Royal*, had a lucky escape that evening: as they closed in on their quarry, they passed within firing distance of Kapitänleutnant Herbert Wohlfarth's *U556*, returning from an Atlantic patrol. The experienced Wohlfarth would not have missed; but he had used up all his torpedoes on British merchant vessels. His inability to take action was almost unbearably galling for Wohlfarth, as *U556*

Above: Under the guns of her destroyer escorts, *Bismarck* lies at anchor in Grimstadfjord. The battleship is sporting blue, white and grey Arctic camouflage, designed to break up her distinctive outline.

and *Bismarck* had exercised together in the Baltic, and he looked on himself as the battleship's protector. Now the *Bismarck*'s last shield had been knocked aside.

Soon after dawn on 27 May, Admiral Tovey closed in from the north-west, his two battleships opening fire at about 0845 hours from a range of 14,600m (16,000 yards). By 1020 hours, the *Bismarck* had been reduced to a blazing wreck, with all her armament out of action, but she was still afloat despite the fact that the two British battleships had fired over 700 shells at her. Only a small proportion had found their target, prompting Admiral Tovey to tell his fleet gunnery officer that he would stand a better chance of hitting her if he threw his binoculars at her. In the end, the battleships, undamaged but seriously short of fuel, were compelled to break off the action, and it was left to the cruisers *Norfolk* and *Dorsetshire* to close in and finish off the *Bismarck* with torpedoes. She sank at 1036 hours, her colours still flying, in position 4810'N, 16°12'W, taking all but 119 of her crew of over 2000 officers and men with her. Her wreck was to lie undisturbed on the ocean floor for nearly half a century, when it was located and photographed by an underwater archaeology expedition, the swastika painted on the warship's bow still clearly visible.

MASSIVE RELIEF

The destruction of the *Bismarck* brought massive relief to the British Government. 'Had she escaped,' Winston Churchill wrote later, 'the morale effects of her continuing existence as

Above: Admiral Lütjens, in command of the fleet from June 1940, faithfully followed Admiral Raeder's instructions on the tactical deployment of the navy's big ships.

Above: Hit by a shell from the *Prince of Wales*, the *Bismarck*'s bows are noticeably lower in the water after the Denmark Strait battle. She was also losing oil. Lütjens now decided to head for Brest.

Right: The last battle: surrounded by shell splashes from HMS *Rodney* and *King George V*, the *Bismarck* burns on the horizon. Several hundred men escaped the wreck, but only 119 were rescued.

much as the material damage she might have inflicted on our shipping would have been calamitous. Many misgivings would have arisen regarding our capacity to control the oceans, and these would have been trumpeted around the world to our great detriment and discomfort.'

The *Prinz Eugen*, meanwhile, had headed south to refuel in mid-Atlantic after parting company with the *Bismarck* on 24 May, but continuing engine defects persuaded Capt Brinkmann to abort his sortie and make for Brest. Although she was sighted by a Coastal Command patrol, she reached harbour unmolested on 1 June, aided by the fact that many British warships were in port refuelling and rearming after the pursuit of the *Bismarck*. For the rest of the year the *Prinz Eugen*, together with the battlecruisers *Scharnhorst* and *Gneisenau*, were immobilized in the Biscay ports, where they were subjected to heavy and costly attacks by RAF bomber Command in which all three suffered damage. As a

further insurance against future sorties by the enemy surface raiders, the Royal Navy began a systematic hunt for their tankers and supply ships after the sinking of the *Bismarck*. In June 1941 five tankers and three supply ships, plus a couple of weather observation vessels, were destroyed or scuttled after being intercepted.

One consequence of the *Bismarck*'s sinking was that the Luftwaffe came in for much criticism for its failure to intervene and attack the British naval forces that were closing in on the battleship. After all, the air force's French bases were well within range of the area of the *Bismarck*'s last battle. The fact is that the Fliegerführer Atlantik (Air Commander Atlantic), Colonel Harlinghausen, had done what he could.

The *Bismarck*

Above: Protection was a key factor in the *Bismarck*'s design. The hull was subdivided into 22 separate watertight compartments and 70 per cent of her waterline length was covered by heavy armour.

On 24 May, when Luftflotte 3's HQ in Paris was apprized of *Bismarck*'s intention to head for St Nazaire, she was still a good two days outside the effective range of the Luftwaffe's Heinkel He 111 and Junkers Ju 88 bombers. On 26 May, the day when contact might have been made, the weather was atrocious, and flying almost impossible. Reconnaisance sorties were flown, however. At 1545 hours, a lone FW 200 Condor sighted the battleship HMS *Rodney*, accompanied by destroyers, but failed to spot the *King George V*, hidden under low cloud. Unlike British long-range reconnaissance aircraft, the Condors as yet carried no radar. The Condor gave the position of the British warships as 1200km (750 miles)

off the French coast, but the likelihood is that they were closer. However, as the combat radius of the German bombers was 885km (550 miles), take-off was ordered for 0300 hours on the morning of 27 May, by which time the *Bismarck*'s fate was sealed.

At 0950 hours, five Ju 88s of Coastal Group 606 arrived over the battle area and tried, without success, to attack British warships. An hour later, with the *Bismarck* already gone, 17 He 111s of I/KG28 from Nantes attacked the *Ark Royal*, but all their bombs missed. In all, 218 sorties were flown by Kampfgruppe 100, II/KG1, II/KG54 and I/KG77 against Force H as it made for Gibraltar; they succeeded only in damaging the destroyer HMS *Mashona*, which sank off the west coast of Ireland on 28 May.

The destruction of the *Bismarck*, and the British blockade of the French Atlantic ports, brought an end to the German Navy's plan to launch a powerful raiding squadron against the British Atlantic convoys. In any case, by the autumn of 1941 the naval planners were now switching their focus to Arctic waters, following the German invasion of Russia. However, Admiral Sir John Tovey, the Commander-in-Chief, Home Fleet, was as yet unaware of this shift in emphasis, and at the beginning of 1942, against the depressing backdrop of Allied reverses in the Far East and North Africa, he had two main anxieties. The first concerned the German Brest Squadron – the *Scharnhorst*, *Gneisenau* and *Prinz Eugen* – now believed to be battleworthy again, and the second arose through the movement of the new and very powerful bat-

Left: Shells from the battleship HMS *Rodney* falling around the *Bismarck*. Expected Luftwaffe air cover did not arrive until after the battleship had been sunk; the bombers lacked sufficient combat radius.

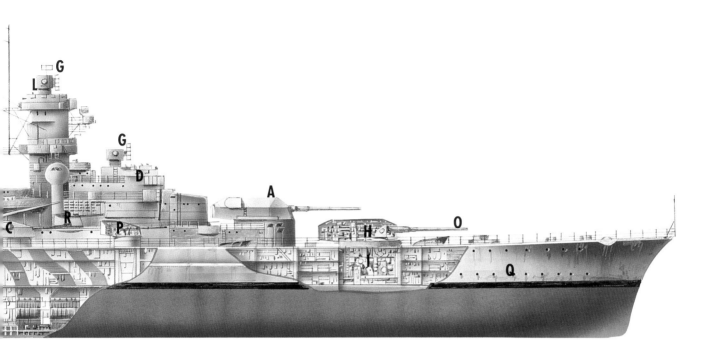

KEY BOX

A   Main gun turrets had 360mm (14in) thick armour on the front, 220mm (8.6in) on the sides and 130mm (5in) on the roof

B   Barbettes for 380mm (15in) gun turrets had 220 (8.6in) armour

C   Secondary battery turret armour ranged from 100mm (3.9in) on the front to 20mm (0.75in) on the roof

D   Conning tower had 200mm (7.8in) thick armoured sides but was knocked out by an 8in shell when theoretically it was proof against battleship gunfire

E   Armour protection on the *Bismarck* was very thorough In spite of being critically damaged in combat in 1941 and no longer able to fight, the vessel was completely intact below the armoured deck, being eventually scuttled by her crew

F   German designers increased the displacement on the *Bismarck,* originally set at 35,561 tonnes (35,000 tons), to cope with the increase in speed of 6 knots and

also to carry extra anti-aircraft armament

G   Seetakt Radar was used mostly for gunnery control and not surface search for enemy vessels

H   Hydraulic mountings for the 380mm (15in) guns were coupled together and fired simultaneously

I   Machinery compartment contained hydraulic pumps, electric motor starters and switchloads plus a back up system using high pressure air for the cylinder heads in case of failing of main supply

J   Triple three bladed 4.7m (15.5ft) diameter screws

K   With twin rudders, *Bismarck* was very responsive in answering the helm but difficult to control at low speeds

L   Optical rangefinder was far superior to many fitted to foreign war ships

M   One fixed transverse mounted double catapult to handle the Arado 196 Floatplane

N   Propulsion was provided by three sets of Blohm and Voss single

reduction geared turbines

O   Main armament comprised 380mm (15in) SKC/34 47 calibre guns each weighing 111 tonnes (109 tons)

P   Secondary armament was 12 150mm (6in) 55C28 guns in twin turrets

Q   *Bismarck's* hull had an extremely broad beam to provide stability making her a very steady gun platform

R   Main A.A. armament comprised 105mm (4in) C65 guns with 80 degree elevation in twin mounts

S   Additional A.A. fire was provided by 16 37mm (1.5in) 83 C30 with a supply of 32,000 rounds backed up by 12 20mm (0.75in) A.A. guns with 24,000 rounds

T   Fuel was housed in large compartments along most of the hull side outboard of boiler and machine spaces. Fuel capacity was 7460 tonnes (7344 tons)

U   12 Wagner Ultra High Pressure Boilers

Above: The battlecruisers *Scharnhorst* and *Gneisenau* photographed in Brest harbour by a Spitfire of the RAF's Photographic Reconnaissance Unit. A smokescreen in being generated to cover the warships.

tleship *Tirpitz* to join the Trondheim Squadron in mid-January, clearly to form the nucleus of a powerful battle group for operations against the Allied Arctic and North Atlantic convoys.

HIGH-SPEED DASH

On 12 January 1942, following a further attack on the three warships at Brest by RAF Bomber Command, Adolf Hitler decided that the vessels must be moved if they were to avoid further damage. Since there was little likelihood that they might break out into the Atlantic unscathed, only two options remained. The first was to return them to Germany by means of a high-speed dash through the English Channel; the second was to decommission them. Faced with such a choice, Vice-Admiral Ciliax, commanding the Brest Squadron, produced an outline plan for a breakout operation, which was allocated the code-name Cerberus. (In Greek mythology, Cerberus was the three-headed dog that guarded the gates of hell). The ships were to leave Brest at night to avoid detection for as long as possible, and then pass through the Straits of Dover in daylight, placing them in a better position to fight off torpedo attacks by surface vessels and aircraft. This

would also let them take full advantage of the strong air umbrella that could be provided by the Luftwaffe.

The British maintained their surveillance of Brest throughout January, and air reconnaisance on the 25th showed that all three ships had left their berths and were in the main harbour. The photographs also showed an increasing number of supporting craft at Brest and concentrations at various Channel ports of S-boats (fast coastal craft known to the British as E-boats).

On 2 February, the Admiralty distributed to all authorities a study of the various options open to the Germans. This concluded that their most probable course of action was a dash through the Channel to their home bases. The main burden of countering this move fell not on the Home Fleet, but on the naval commands at Plymouth, Portsmouth and Dover – especially on the latter, whose forces were most favourably placed for interception. As a preliminary step the Admiralty ordered certain redeployments of destroyers, submarines, minelayers and MTBs (motor torpedo boats). To supplement these forces, six Swordfish of No. 825 Squadron, Fleet Air Arm, were deployed to Manston in Kent on 4 February; every available aircraft of Bomber Command was bombed-up and placed on two hours' readiness; No. 19 Group of Coastal Command stepped up its surveillance of the southwestern approaches; and Fighter Command stood ready to provide air cover. After a week, however, the state of readiness was downgraded and squadrons released for other operations, with the proviso that they would immediately be switched to anti-shipping operations if necessary.

FRENCH RESISTANCE

On 8 February, British Intelligence received a warning from the French Resistance that the warships were making ready to sail, and subsequent air reconnaissance showed the *Scharnhorst* and *Prinz Eugen* in the harbour and the *Gneisenau* just outside. Armed with this knowledge, and with information to the effect that weather conditions would be favourable for a breakout within 48 hours, the Admiralty and Air Ministry concluded that the Germans would make their attempt during the week beginning 10 February. On the 11th, air reconnaissance revealed that the three warships were once again in the main harbour, with six destroyers and a concentration of smaller craft. RAF Bomber Command carried out a small-scale attack during the night, but its only result was to delay the start of the breakout by an hour.

The ships eventually formed up in the roads outside Brest at 2245 hours, and now began an unfortunate chain of circumstances that was to deprive the British of vital intelligence of their movements. A French Resistance agent saw them sail, but was unable to reach his transmitter because of a strong security cordon around the harbour. A Coastal Command Hudson patrol aircraft had to return early with radar failure, and its replacement detected nothing at all, even though the enemy ships were well within range of its ASV (Air to Surface Vessel) radar. No replacement arrived to cover the gap left by this aircraft, and the fact that this stretch of the coastline was no longer being watched was not reported to the Admiralty. In fact, the third Hudson patrol had been recalled because of fog; if it had reached its station, patrolling an area off the Sussex coast, it would almost certainly have detected the ships at first light.

Below: Surrounded by support vessels and flak ships, *Prinz Eugen* is located by a reconnaissance aircraft in Hjelte Fjord, Norway, on 21 February 1942, shortly before making a sortie into the Norwegian Sea.

Right: With her rudders jury-rigged and operated manually, *Prinz Eugen* heads for Trondheim after receiving a heavy hit in the stern from a torpedo fired by the submarine HMS *Trident*, 23 February 1942.

By that time, the Brest Squadron was steaming at full speed off Barfleur, following a channel swept by eight minesweeping flotillas in the preceding weeks and escorted by six destroyers. At the narrowest stretch of the Channel, between Le Havre and Dunkirk, the force was to be strengthened by fourteen vessels of the 2nd, 3rd and 5th Torpedo-Boat Flotillas, while the 2nd and 6th S-boat Flotillas were to join the escort in the North Sea. Air Fleet 3 had allocated 176 bombers and fighters (mainly the Me109s and FW190s of JGs 2 and 26) to the operation, covering the force with relays of at least 16 aircraft at all times.

RADIO SILENCE

For almost 13 hours, the Brest Squadron continued its passage up the Channel unmolested, even though it had been sighted by the pilots of two sections of patrolling Spitfires, at least one of whom broke radio silence to report the warships' position. The subsequent slowness of the British reaction can be explained only by a communications breakdown somewhere along the line. It must be said, however, that the German ships were greatly helped by the weather conditions, which effectively ruled out air attack at this time. The Royal Navy's surface units were also poorly placed for an attack; the destroyers were exercising in the North Sea, and the small force of MTBs at Ramsgate had suffered in an engagement during the night.

At 1120 hours, the German force reduced speed to ten knots to allow sweepers to clear a path through the minefield laid by British destroyers. The passage took 20 minutes and the ships once again went ahead at full speed; an ideal opportunity to attack them during the interval had been lost. At 1218 hours, the gun batteries at Dover became the first units to try to engage the enemy and opened fire on the warships, but their shells fell short. At the same time, five MTBs from Dover under Lt Cdr Pumphrey began their attack run, heading for the outer screen of torpedo-boats and the destroyers beyond, the latter laying a smoke screen. The battlecruisers were visible beyond the smoke and Pumphrey

Left: Taken from the *Prinz Eugen*, this photograph shows the *Scharnhorst*, followed by the *Gneisenau*, heading at speed through the English Channel on 12 February 1942. The British were caught off guard.

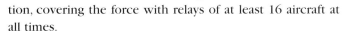

signalled their position, speed and course – information that was relayed to the MTBs at Ramsgate and the Fleet Air Arm detachment at Manston. Bereft of any support from fighter-bombers or MGBs, both of which had been promised, Pumphrey's small force tried to slip through the escort screen. Intense fire from the escort vessels and from enemy aircraft forced the MTBs to split up and make individual attacks; most of their torpedoes were launched at a range of two miles or more, and no hits were observed.

SPITFIRE ESCORT

Meanwhile, alerted by the MTBs' signals, the six Swordfish of No 825 Squadron had taken off from Manston at 1225 hours. They were led by Lieutenant-Commander Eugene Esmonde, who had been promised an escort of five Spitfire squadrons. However, a combination of bad weather and a timing error resulted in only ten Spitfires turning up three minutes after the Swordfish had set course. Within ten minutes, the Spitfires were engaged in a fierce low-level battle with enemy fighters, in the course of which they lost contact with the Swordfish. The latter, flying in two sections of three, pressed on unescorted towards the warships, harassed by fighters all the way. The pilots of the first three Swordfish selected the *Scharnhorst* as they broke through the outer screen and launched their torpedoes. Esmonde went down into the sea immediately afterwards and the other two Swordfish were forced down within a minute or so, five of their six crew members later being picked up alive by the MTBs. The second flight of Swordfish was seen passing over the torpedo-boat screen, then the three aircraft vanished in the smoke and the geysers of water flung up by the cruisers' armament: all three were shot down and their crews killed. Of the 18 crew involved in the operation, only five survived. Lieutenant-Commander Esmonde, who had

Left: Lt Cdr G.M.F. Fuller, the *Dorsetshire's* gunnery officer. *Bismarck* survivors contended their ship sank because she was scuttled, and not because of *Dorsetshire's* torpedoes.

Beaufort torpedo bombers were fragmented and produced no result. In all, the RAF lost 41 aircraft, including seventeen fighters; the Luftwaffe's losses amounted to seventeen aircraft.

BRITISH MINEFIELD

The assault by the first wave of bombers coincided with an attempted attack by six destroyers from Harwich, HMS *Campbell*, *Mackay*, *Vivacious*, *Worcester*, *Whitshed* and *Walpole*, led by Captains C.T.M. Pizey and J.P. Wright. The *Walpole* developed mechanical trouble and returned to Harwich, leaving the other five to execute the attack. It was a hazardous operation; not only did the destroyer crews have to contend with enemy fire, but they also had to thread their way through a British minefield and run the gauntlet of British bombs. The ships reached the outer screen at about 1530 hours and initiated individual attacks on the *Gneisenau* and other vessels, but intense fire from the battlecruisers' heavy armament kept the destroyers at arm's length and they were forced to launch their torpedoes at long range. Only one destroyer, HMS *Worcester*, came within 2700m (3000 yards); she was badly damaged and set on fire, limping back to Harwich with four of her crew dead and 19 wounded and coming close to being attacked by a Beaufort en route. Once again, the German warships were unharmed.

The Brest Squadron slipped away into the darkness. Just before 2000 hours, the *Gneisenau* struck a mine, but sustained no very serious injury. Ninety minutes later, however, the *Scharnhorst* was mined a second time and came to a stop, but by that time the British had lost touch with the enemy and were unable to take advantage of this development. On 13 February, the *Scharnhorst* limped to safety in Wilhelmshaven while the other two warships went on to the Elbe Estuary.

The 'Channel Dash' had been an undisputed success for the Germans, and for the British a woeful tale of incompetence, bad planning and humiliation, for which not even the courage of the Royal Navy and RAF could compensate, and which went a long way towards wiping out the elation that had been experienced at the sinking of the *Bismarck*. Yet for the enemy, the sequel to the operation was not a happy one. The *Gneisenau* was hit by Bomber Command in Kiel harbour a fortnight after Cerberus and never went to sea again; her gun turrets were removed for coastal defence and she was sunk as a blockship at Gdynia, where she was seized by the Russians and broken up between 1947 and 1951.

The *Scharnhorst*, out of action for the time being, would emerge once more to menace Allied convoys in northern waters. *Prinz Eugen*, too, would fight again, but only in the Baltic.

There remained the *Tirpitz*.

not expected to return, was posthumously awarded the Victoria Cross.

RISING SEAS

It was now 1300 hours and the warships, still unscathed, were passing Ramsgate, from where three MTBs under Lt Cdr Long set out to attack them. Like their colleagues at Dover, they found the enemy's defensive screen too strong to penetrate and they were soon left behind, returning to harbour in rapidly deteriorating weather and rising seas. But trouble for the Brest Squadron was not far over the horizon: at 1421 hours, the *Scharnhorst* struck a mine while passing at reduced speed through another dangerous bottleneck – the Ruytingen Narrows. Her engines were temporarily stopped and it was half an hour before she could get under way – half an hour during which not a single British aircraft was sighted. Admiral Ciliax and his staff were transferred to the leading destroyer by cutter, only to be transferred again when the warship was damaged by the premature explosion of one of its own shells.

At about 1445 hours, aircraft of Bomber Command arrived overhead, and before nightfall the Command had flown 242 sorties against the ships, although only one in six managed to bomb them. They succeeded in sinking the patrol ship V1302 and in damaging the torpedo boats T13 and Jaguar. Attacks by

Left: Exhausted survivors of the *Bismarck* being rescued by the cruiser HMS *Dorsetshire*. Many had to be left in the water because of the threat posed by U-boats believed to be in the vicinity.

CHAPTER 4

Tirpitz: The Last Battleship

Formidable though she was, the *Tirpitz* was never used aggressively – and she never put to sea if an aircraft carrier was in the vicinity.

The *Tirpitz*, the *Bismarck*'s sister ship, was launched at Wilhelmshaven on 1 April 1939, in the presence of Adolf Hitler, by the daughter of Grossadmiral Alfred von Tirpitz himself, who had died a little under a decade earlier. This was Frau von Hassel, wife of the German Ambassador to Rome (who was later implicated in the July 1944 bomb plot against Hitler and executed). On the night of 19–20 July 1940, the *Tirpitz* and the heavy cruiser *Admiral Scheer* were unsuccessfully attacked by the RAF in Wilhelmshaven naval dockyard. Completed in February 1941, she went to Gotenhafen to begin her sea trials. Early results proved so encouraging that, when Hitler visited the battleships there on 5 May 1941, the *Tirpitz*'s commander, Captain Topp, begged permission to accompany the *Bismarck* on her Atlantic sortie. Hitler made no reply.

After completion of her trials in the autumn of 1941, the *Tirpitz* was designated flagship of the German Baltic Fleet, which was then commanded by Vice-Admiral Ciliax. In September 1941 she led a powerful battle group comprising the heavy cruiser *Admiral Scheer*, the cruisers *Köln* and *Nürnberg*, three destroyers, five torpedo boats and a flotilla of S-boats that sailed north to the mouth of the Gulf of Finland to counter a possible breakout into the Baltic by the Soviet Fleet; in the event this never happened, the Russian warships having been subjected to fierce air attack at Kronstadt, their principal base.

Towards the end of October, British Naval Intelligence received indications that the *Tirpitz* was about to break out into the Atlantic. As an insurance against this, Admiral Tovey positioned units south of Iceland and in the Denmark Strait. These included the battleship *King George V*, the aircraft carrier *Victorious*, three heavy and two light cruisers – all from the Home Fleet – and an American battle squadron comprising the battleships USS *Idaho* and *Mississippi* and two

Left: Built at the Wilhelmshaven Navy Yard, the *Tirpitz* – seen here after launching – was similar in construction and appearance to her sister ship the *Bismarck*, but had a greater displacement and could carry more fuel.

cruisers. Although the United States were not yet at war with Germany, the US Navy had been participating in Atlantic convoy escort work since August 1941, following a vital meeting between Winston Churchill and US President Franklin D. Roosevelt.

LONG VOYAGE

It was not until the night of 16 January 1942, however, that the *Tirpitz* left her home port of Wilhelmshaven for the last time, flying the flag of Admiral Ciliax and under the command of Captain Topp. Her destination was Trondheim, in Norway, and the decision that she should go there on her first long voyage had been ratified by Hitler himself at a meeting with Admiral Raeder in December 1941. It was based on two considerations; the first was Hitler's concern that the British might attempt a landing in northern Norway, and the second was a shortage of fuel oil, which greatly reduced her radius of action and prevented her from being sent out on long sorties into the Atlantic. From now on the Arctic was to be her hunting-ground, and the Allied convoys of supplies to Russia her quarry.

But there was also a strategic plan, outlined by Raeder at a further meeting with Hitler just before the *Tirpitz* sailed.

Above: The *Tirpitz* at anchor in Altenfjord. This well-protected inlet, close to the extreme northern tip of Norway, provided an ideal base for sorties against Allied convoys heading to and from the Kola Peninsula.

The ship's strategic function was to protect the German position in the Norwegian and Arctic areas by threatening the flank of enemy operations against northern Norway, by attacking the White Sea convoys, and by tying down strong enemy forces in the Atlantic to prevent reinforcement of the Mediterranean, the Indian Ocean and the Pacific. This could be done to some degree by keeping the *Tirpitz* ready for action in Trondheim, but the best results would only be obtained by offensive sorties.

Hitler was obsessed, as indeed was Winston Churchill, with the strategic importance of Norway, and was convinced that the British were about to attempt a landing there; so convinced was he, in fact, that, on 14 January, he ordered a U-boat group codenamed 'Schlei' (Tench), en route to its patrol stations in the Atlantic, to redeploy to an area west of the Hebrides and Faeroes, ready to intercept any invasion force heading for Norway from the Clyde. Hitler had expressed his fears to Raeder at the December 1941 meeting:

'If the British go about things properly they will attack northern Norway at several points. By means of an all-out attack with their fleet and landing troops, they will try to displace us there, take Narvik if possible and thus exert pressure on Sweden and Finland. This might be of decisive importance for the outcome of the war.'

It was the first time since the war began that Hitler had conceded the possibility that there might be any outcome other than total German victory; and it was his fear about Norway that led him to risk the Brest Squadron in the epic dash through the English Channel on 12 February 1942.

HEAVY HIT

Only one of the three warships that managed to break out, the *Prinz Eugen*, remained seaworthy. On 21 February 1942, still under the command of Captain Brinkmann, she left Brunsbüttel with the heavy cruiser *Admiral Scheer* and the destroyers *Z25*, *Hermann Schoemann* and *Friedrich Ihn* to join the *Tirpitz* in Norway. The force was unsuccessfully attacked as it passed through the North Sea, two RAF aircraft being shot down, but on 23 February the British submarine *Trident* obtained a heavy hit on her stern as she approached Trondheim. After emergency repairs there, she left for Germany on 16 May. The next day she was attacked by 12 Beaufort torpedo-bombers and six Blenheims; the attack was unsuccessful, three aircraft being lost to anti-aircraft fire and fighters. Four

Below: The *Prinz Eugen* undergoing emergency repairs at Trondheim after being hit in the stern by a torpedo from HM submarine *Trident* on 23 February 1942. Note the boom defences (anti-torpedo netting).

Left: HMS *Renown* seen off the coast of Gibraltar. In March 1942, *Renown* formed part of a fleet of battleships, cruisers and destroyers which tracked and hunted down the *Tirpitz.*

Navy to swallow, but it did have one result; on Hitler's orders, the *Tirpitz* never put to sea again if carrier-based aircraft were known to be in the vicinity.

On 11 March, the battleship entered Narvik, and the following day she sailed for Trondheim, evading a force of British destroyers that tried to intercept her off Bodo. On 30 March, RAF Bomber Command mounted its first attempt in strength on the warship, but the 34 Handley Page Halifax bombers sent out to Trondheim failed to locate the *Tirpitz*. One aircraft failed to return.

The British Admiralty, meanwhile, was still seriously concerned that the *Tirpitz* and other powerful surface units that were assembling in Norway might be preparing for a sortie into the Atlantic. As far back as the previous August, Admiral Sir Dudley Pound, then First Sea Lord, had been making plans to

more aircraft were shot down by fighters during subsequent attacks. The warship eventually arrived at Kiel for major repair on 18 May, destined to spend the rest of her war in the Baltic.

Meanwhile, on 6 March 1942, the *Tirpitz*, accompanied by three destroyers, set out to intercept convoys PQ12 and QP8, the first bound for Murmansk, the second on its way home. The day before, a FW 200 had detected PQ12 130km (70nm) south of Jan Mayen Island, and the submarines *U134*, *U377*, *U403* and *U584* were also deployed to intercept it. At the same time, however, the movements of the *Tirpitz* and her escorts had been reported by the submarine *Seawolf*. Units of the Home Fleet, comprising the battleships *King George V*, *Duke of York* and *Renown*, the carrier *Victorious*, the cruiser *Kenya* and 12 destroyers placed themselves between the threat and the convoys, which passed one another off Bear Island at noon on 7 March. Ciliax detached some of his destroyers to search for the convoys and they sank one straggling Russian freighter, but apart from that no contact was made and the German commander turned southwards again.

BITTER PILL

Thanks to intercepted radio signals, Admiral Tovey knew of the Germans' intentions and ordered his forces towards the Lofoten Islands in an attempt to cut them off. At daybreak on the 9th, a reconnaissance Albacore from the *Victorious* spotted the *Tirpitz*, and 12 torpedo-carrying Fairey Albacores took off soon afterwards to attack the warship. The attack, unfortunately, was carried out in line astern, which gave the *Tirpitz* ample room to avoid all the torpedoes, although one passed within 10m (30ft) of her. Two Albacores were shot down. The failure of this attack was a bitter pill for the Royal

Below: The men who led the hunt for Germany's battleships: Prime Minister Winston S. Churchill, and the First Sea Lord, Admiral Sir Dudley Pound. The strong resolve of both men produced results.

deal with such an eventuality by keeping two King George V class battleships available at all times. In practice, this meant that three had to be kept in home waters in case one was out of action for any reason. To keep an effective watch on the *Tirpitz*, and to launch an air strike against her if she left Trondheim, meant that an aircraft carrier also had to be retained in home waters. In effect, therefore, four British capital ships were tied down by one German battleship, with the latter – for the moment at least – doing nothing more than ride at anchor in a Norwegian fjord.

RAM AND DESTROY

One way of discouraging such an Atlantic sortie was to make it impossible for the *Tirpitz* to dock in western France. This meant putting out of action the facilities at St Nazaire, which featured the only dry dock capable of handling her. Known as the Normandie lock through its association with the famous French passenger liner, or more correctly the Forme Ecluse, it was over 335m (1100ft) in length; and it was towards this haven that the *Bismarck* would have headed had she not been sunk in 1941. The principal objective of the plan to raid St Nazaire, code-named Operation Chariot, was to ram and destroy the lock gates of the Forme Ecluse using the old destroyer HMS

Above: An air reconnaissance photograph showing the destroyer HMS *Campbeltown*, her bows torn away, lying in the dry dock at St Nazaire. This audacious raid effectively kept the *Tirpitz* out of the Atlantic.

Campbeltown (formerly USS *Buchanan*), her bows filled with explosives; the destruction of the smaller South Lock gates and their installations, pumping machinery for the outer dock, and any U-boats or shipping present, were to be subsidiary objectives in that order of priority. The Naval Force comprised the *Campbeltown*, two escorting Hunt class destroyers, *Atherstone* and *Tynedale*, a motor gunboat, a motor torpedo boat and 15 motor launches, four of which carried torpedoes and the remainder the Military Force, consisting of 44 officers and 224 other ranks of No. 2 Commando and detachments from others. The Naval Force commander was Commander R.E.D. Ryder, RN, in peacetime an Arctic explorer and winner of the Polar Medal, while the Military Force was commanded by Lietenant-Colonel A.C. Newman of the Essex Regiment.

The military plan of attack was based on landings at three places, from the bows of the *Campbeltown*, from motor launches on either side of the Old Entrance, and on

the north side of the Old Mole. Demolition parties assigned to the three assault groups were to concentrate the destruction of the bridges, which would effectively turn the area into an island. The force was then to withdraw to the Old Mole for re-embarkation. Two hours was the maximum time allowed for the Military Force to complete its operation, by which time the Naval Force would have to leave in order to get clear before daybreak and rejoin the escorting destroyers.

The expedition sailed from Falmouth at 1400 hours on Tuesday 26 March 1942, led by HMS *Atherstone*, towing MGB 314. Astern of her came HMS *Campbeltown*, towing MTB 74. Next in line was HMS *Tynedale*, with the MLs forming two columns on either side of the destroyers.

U-BOAT

The outward trip was not without incident. At 0720 hours on 27 March, Tynedale sighted a U-boat on the surface at 3675m (4000 yards) and opened fire as she closed, forcing the submarine to crash-dive. The U-boat's periscope was seen shortly afterwards and it appeared that she might have been damaged, but Tynedale's captain, Lt Cdr D. Tweedie, decided against ramming for fear of damaging his own ship and instead dropped a pattern of depth charges. The U-boat's bow and conning tower emerged from the water and Tynedale engaged her with 101.6mm (4-inch) and automatic weapons. The submarine assumed a 40-degree list to port and disappeared stern first. No further contact was made with the submarine, but it was by no means certain that it had been destroyed. (In fact, no U-boat was reported lost on this day at this location). Later, two French trawlers were encountered and sunk by gunfire after their crews had been taken off.

Just after 1700 hours on the 27th, the force received a signal from the Commander-in-Chief, Plymouth, saying that five S-boats were believed to be operating in the area. (In reality this was the 5th Torpedo-Boat Flotilla, comprising the TBs *Falke*, *Iltis*, *Kondor*, *Jaguar* and *Seeadler*). Two hours later, another signal informed the force commander that two more Hunt class destroyers, the *Cleveland* and *Brocklesby*, were being sent at maximum speed as reinforcements. During the afternoon the force had been following a decoy route across the Bay of Biscay towards La Pallice and La Rochelle, but now it turned north-east and headed for St Nazaire at 15 knots. At 0045 hours on 28

Above: HMS *Campbeltown* being examined by German personnel as she lies wedged in the lock gates. A short time later, she exploded. Note the shell damage to her side.

March, the force was within sight of the north bank of the Loire; by this time the two escorting destroyers had parted company and were patrolling to seaward.

RAF BOMBERS

The fact that the expedition arrived at exactly the right place at the right time was a tribute to the navigational skill of Lieutenant A.R. Green, RN, the Force Navigation Officer. The vessels now began their final approach, with three Coastal Force craft – *MGB314* and two MLs – ahead of the *Campbeltown* and *MTB74* and two columns of MLs astern. By now a small number of RAF bombers had arrived overhead to create a diversion and the St Nazaire flak defences were putting up a fine barrage.

As the force came abeam Les Morees Tower, 5km (3 miles) from the town, a single searchlight swept the estuary and a challenge came from a German shore station. *MGB314* replied with a false identification, followed by a signal in German that she was 'proceeding up harbour in accordance with previous instructions'. The bluff seemed to have worked; then, with 1.6km (2 miles) to run, the searchlights came on again, fixing on the Campbeltown, and the defences opened up.

The force increased speed, returning fire as it forged ahead, and at 0134 hours the bows of the *Campbeltown*, with their five tons of explosive, slammed into the lock gates and stuck fast. While the commandos on board her streamed ashore to carry out their demolition tasks, a party of naval engineers under Chief Engine Room Artificer H. Howard set about flooding the ship. This part of the operation had been accomplished with fine precision, and it later brought the award of the Victoria Cross to the *Campbeltown*'s captain, Lieutenant-Commander S.H. Beattie, RN.

UNARMOURED HULLS

The MLs, meanwhile, had been having a difficult time, some having been hit and set on fire as they struggled to land their troops. The port column, heading for the Old Mole, suffered particularly severely as gunfire ripped through their unarmoured hulls. The leading craft, *ML447*, got to within 3m (10ft) of the jetty before she was set ablaze by machine gun fire and grenades; her commander, Lt T.D.L. Platt, RNR, persisted in his attempts to land until *ML160* arrived. The latter's skipper, Lt T.W. Boyd, RNVR, placed his craft between the Mole and ML447 and took off some survivors, including Platt. Both officers were subsequently awarded the DSO. Some time later, ML160 was joined by *ML443* and *ML446*; they were the only three MLs to return to England under their own power and without escort.

Meanwhile, *MTB74* had torpedoed the gates of the submarine pens and *MGB314*, with the Force commanders on board, had been engaging enemy gun positions from a point midstream. Able Seaman W.A. Savage, the layer of the MGB's Pom-Pom, did excellent work amid all the fury and flying metal; he was killed by a shell splinter during the withdrawal, and was awarded a posthumous VC. (The other posthumous VC went to Sergeant J.F. Durrant of the Royal Engineers).

Many of the *Campbeltown*'s crew were also rescued by *MGB314*, and afterwards Commander Ryder gave the order to withdraw; he also received a VC for his part in the night's

work. HMS *Tynedale* engaged incoming boats of the German 5th TB Flotilla outside the harbour while a severely decimated force fought its way out of the Loire estuary to make rendezvous with the escorting destroyers. Of the 62 naval officers and 291 ratings who had sailed from England, 34 officers and 151 ratings were killed or missing, and of the total of 44 officers and 224 other ranks of No. 2 Commando, 34 officers and 178 other ranks never returned. In fact, it was not until much later that the true casualty figures were established; 170 men killed or missing out of 621 committed. Given the nature of the operation, it was a remarkably light price to pay for the denial to the enemy of a major and threatening naval facility.

Shortly before noon on 28 March, Cambeltown's demolition charges blew up with devastating effect. The lock gate was blown off its sill and seriously damaged, and the dock itself was put out of commission for the rest of the war.

SECOND ATTACK

On the night of 27–28 April 1942, the *Tirpitz* was subjected to a second air attack at Trondheim, this time by 31 Halifaxes and 12 Lancasters. No hits were scored, and four Halifaxes and a Lancaster were shot down. A fifth Halifax (W1048 of No. 35 Squadron), damaged by flak, made a forced landing on the frozen Lake Hoklingen and sank gently. It was a new aircraft on its first mission and all the crew survived. The remains of this aircraft were recovered in 1982 and are now on display in the Royal Air Force Museum at Hendon, London.

The fact that the *Tirpitz* remained at Trondheim after her sortie in March was largely because of a shortage of fuel oil. The March sortie had used up over 8130 tonnes (8000 tons),

Below: While in harbour at Trondheim, the *Tirpitz* was subjected to air attack by both RAF and Russian bombers.

The *Tirpitz*

KEY BOX

1. Rudder
2. Steering engine
3. Screws
4. 20mm (0.7in) and 37mm (1.5in) anti-aircraft guns
5. 380mm (14.9in) guns
6. Sighting hood
7. Passage
8. Auxiliary dynamo room
9. Electricians' stores
10. Food storage
11. Dynamo
12. Cold store
13. Engineers' quarters
14. Engineers' stores
15. Shaft
16. Reduction gear
17. Rangefinder for secondary armament
18. Radar
19. Aft control position
20. Armoured access tube to control
21. Ship's stores
22. Twin 102mm (4in) guns
23. Twin 150mm (5.9in) guns
24. Storage platform for lifeboats
25. Lookout post
26. Turbines
27. Engine control centre
28. Double bottom
29. Boilers
30. Ventilators
31. Small boat crane
32. Searchlight
33. Rangefinder for main guns
34. Main crane
35. Armoured upper (spotting) bridge
36. Navigation bridge
37. Admiral's bridge
38. Plotting room
39. Main control centre
40. Bridge
41. Breech of 150mm (5.9in) gun
42. Turntable of 150mm (5.9in) gun
43. Machinery for turning turret
44. Armoured housing for turret machinery
45. 150mm (5.9in) ammunition
46. 100mm (3.9in)-thick sloping armoured deck
47. Watertight compartments (partly used for fuel storage)
48. Wing passages
49. 320mm (12.5in)-thick side armour
50. 270mm (10.6in)-thick side armour (reducing to 145mm (5.7in) at top)
51. Paravane sweep
52. Ventilation shaft to turret working areas
53. Barbette
54. Medical centre
55. Crew
56. 380mm (14.9in) magazine
57. Loading tray for 380mm (14.9in) gun
58. Cradle for 380mm (14.9in) gun
59. Chase of 380mm (14.9in) gun
60. Turntable
61. Ammunition hoist
62. Loading room
63. Trim tanks
64. Fuel tanks
65. Turntable/elevation machinery
66. Auxiliary/turntable machinery
67. 380mm (14.9in) reserve magazine
68. Crew messing area
69. Clothes issuing store
70. Capstan machinery
71. Capstan
72. Boatswain's stores
73. Galley
74. Main anchor bed
75. Bow anchor

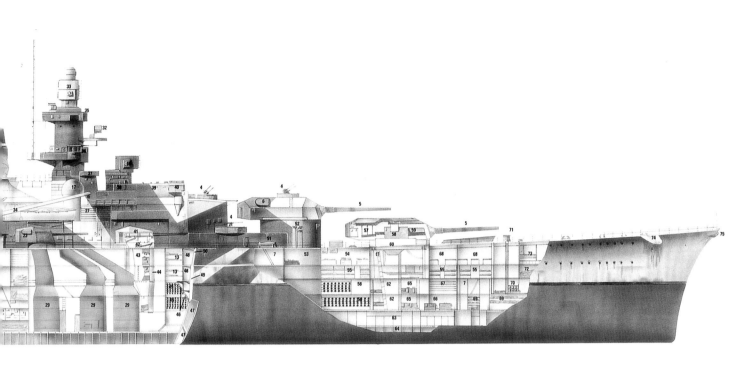

and it was not until early in July that another supply of 16260 tonnes (16,000 tons) was made available, permitting the Trondheim Squadron to put to sea again.

KNIGHT'S MOVE

This windfall coincided with the departure for Russia of the Allied convoy PQ17. On 27 June 1942, it had sailed from Iceland with 36 freighters, protected by a close support

Below: The German heavy cruiser *Admiral Scheer* was part of the German Navy's Trondheim Squadron in 1942. A successful commerce raider, she sank 17 ships in the Atlantic and Indian Oceans in 1940–41.

Above: The mighty *Tirpitz* would certainly have caused much destruction had she operated aggressively against the Allied Arctic convoys, but she never did for fear of air attack.

force and a cover group of four cruisers and three destroyers. Additional long-range support was provided by a cover force from the Home Fleet, consisting of the battleships HMS *Duke of York* and USS *Washington* (the latter attached to Admiral Tovey's command), the carrier *Victorious*, two cruisers and 14 destroyers. As soon as they learned of PQ17's departure, the German Navy initiated Operation Rösselsprung (Knight's Move), its aim the total destruction of

Left: A clear and detailed photograph of the *Tirpitz* in Narvikfjord. The protective torpedo nets are clearly visible. Despite such precautions, midget submarines were able to attack her.

the convoy. In the afternoon of 2 July, Force I set out from Trondheim under the command of Admiral Schniewind; it comprised the *Tirpitz* and the cruiser *Admiral Hipper*, with four destroyers and two torpedo boats. The next day Vice-Admiral Kummetz's Force II, comprising the heavy cruisers *Lützow* and *Admiral Scheer*, with five destroyers, sailed from Narvik and headed north to join Force I at Altenfjord. There they waited, the German commanders unwilling to risk their ships until they had more information about the strength of the enemy's covering forces.

SLAUGHTER

Attacks by torpedo aircraft on the convoy began on 4 July. On the evening of the same day, the Admiralty received a completely false report that a Russian submarine had sighted the German warships heading on an

Below: A British midget submarine during training on a Scottish loch. This particular craft, *X8*, was lost in passage to attack the Tirpitz on 21 September 1943. The warship was damaged by *X6* and *X7* in Altenfjord.

interception course. This, in addition to reports that the convoy was being continually shadowed by enemy aircraft, led to one of the most tragic decisions of the war: to withdraw the escorting cruisers and destroyers and to scatter the convoy, the merchantmen making their way individually to the Russian ports. It was the signal for packs of enemy aircraft and U-boats to fall on the hapless transports and pick them off one by one. The slaughter began on 5 July and went on for five days, right up to the moment when the surviving ships entered Archangel. The convoy's losses were 24 ships out of 36, totalling 146,288 tonnes (143,977 tons). The losses in equipment were astronomical: 3350 vehicles, 430 tanks, 210 aircraft and 100,910 tonnes (99,316) tons of other war equipment. German losses, in over 200 sorties flown by the Luftwaffe, were just five aircraft.

The *Tirpitz* did not sortie from Altenfjord until 5 July. She made no contact with the enemy, although she had a narrow escape when a Soviet submarine, the K21, fired a salvo of torpedoes at her, which missed.

X-CRAFT

The *Tirpitz* remained inactive during the remainder of 1942 and the spring of 1943. Despite this, the presence of the battleship and other heavy units, strategically placed in northern Norway, persuaded the Allies to suspend convoys to Russia during the Arctic summer, when the cover of darkness was stripped away. Desperate measures to eliminate the *Tirpitz* were called for. In August 1943, plans were laid to attack her with four-man midget submarines known as X-craft; these were to be towed across the North Sea by specially modified submarines, then make the final run to the battleship under their own power, and lay explosive charges under her.

The final preparations for the attack were well under way when air reconnaissance revealed that the *Tirpitz* had left Altenfjord on 6 September. In fact, she had sailed at the head of a task force, comprising the *Scharnhorst* and nine destroyers, to bombard Allied bases on Spitzbergen. While the warships destroyed coastal batteries, the destroyers landed a battalion of the 349th Grenadier Regiment, the troops blowing up coal and supply dumps,

Right: This photograph, taken six days after the successful attack by X-craft on 22 September 1943, shows (left) the damaged *Tirpitz* with a number of smaller craft alongside. Thick oil covers the anchorage.

water and electricity stations before withdrawing. It was the only occasion on which *Tirpitz*'s main armament was used against a surface target.

PATROL LINE

The *Scharnhorst* had been in Norwegian waters since March 1943, but apart from the Spitzbergen sortie had been mainly inactive. She did not put to sea again until December, and this time her mission was to engage the Allied Arctic convoys. She was now under the command of Captain F. Hintze and flying the flag of Admiral Bey, a former commodore of destroyers who had recently been appointed to command the Northern Battle Group. At 1400 hours on Christmas Day 1943, the *Scharnhorst* sailed from Norway accompanied by five destroyers to intercept *JW55B*, which had been located by air reconnaissance on 22 December. The convoy had already been attacked by Ju 88s and by U-boats, but without success. On 26 December, Admiral Bey ordered his destroyers to form a patrol line to search for the convoy in heavy seas. He knew that a British cruiser covering force comprising the *Belfast*, *Norfolk* and *Sheffield* was operating in the Barents Sea; what he did not know was that there was also a distant covering force commanded by the Commander-in-Chief Home Fleet, Admiral Sir Bruce Fraser, and comprising the battleship *Duke of York*, the cruiser *Jamaica* and four destroyers, which had sailed from Iceland.

Above: The battlecruiser *Scharnhorst* opens fire with her main armament. The *Scharnhorst* was battered into a blazing hulk off Norway's North Cape on 26 December 1943, while on a sortie to attack a convoy.

Fraser, aware that *JW55B* had been located by enemy aircraft, was convinced that the *Scharnhorst* would make a sortie against it, and detached four detroyers from Convoy RA55A, which he did not consider to be under immediate threat, to reinforce *JW55B*'s close escort. His hope was that this strengthened destroyer force would not only be sufficient to drive off the *Scharnhorst*, but might perhaps dam-

age her enough for the *Duke of York* to come up and finish her off. At this point Fraser's ships were 370km (200nm) south-west of North Cape and the cruiser force, under Admiral Burnett, 278km (150nm) to the east.

SIGNALLING ERROR

Admiral Bey's five destroyers, meanwhile, had not only failed to locate the convoy; they had also, because of a signalling error, lost touch with the flagship and were subsequently ordered to return to base, so that they took no part in the coming events. At 0840 hours on the 26th, the cruisers *Norfolk* and *Belfast* obtained radar contact with the Scharnhorst at 32,000m (35,000 yards), and at 0921 hours the Sheffield glimpsed her in the stormy darkness at 11,895m (13,000 yards). A few minutes later, all three destroyers opened fire on the battlecruiser and obtained three hits, one of which put her port 15cm (6in) fire control system out of action. The *Scharnhorst* replied with a few harmless 28cm (11in) salvoes, then Bey turned away to the south-east while Burnett placed his cruisers between the threat and the convoy, screened by four destroyers from the escort.

Below: The German Navy's Commander of Battleships, Admiral Ciliax, inspecting the crew of the *Scharnhorst*, accompanied by Captain Hoffmann (right). *Scharnhorst* was a constant menace to Allied convoys.

Above: Blindfolded survivors of the *Scharnhorst*, in merchant seamen's rescue kit, being taken ashore at a British port on their way to a prisoner-of-war camp. Their rescuers treated them with kindness.

At 1221 hours, the three cruisers again sighted the *Scharnhorst* and opened fire with full broadsides at 10,065m (11,000 yards), while the destroyers fanned out to attack with torpedoes. Before they were able to get into position, the battlecruiser retired to the north-east, her gunfire having put one of the *Norfolk*'s turrets and all her radar out of action; Sheffield also suffered some splinter damage. But the Scharnhorst had taken punishment too, including a hit abreast 'A' turret and one on her quarterdeck.

EXCELLENT GUNNERY

At 1617 hours, the *Duke of York*, now 37km (20nm) away to the north-northeast, obtained a radar echo from the Scharnhorst. At 1650 hours, Fraser ordered the *Belfast* to illuminate her with starshell, and immediately afterwards the *Duke of York* opened fire with her 35.5cm (14in) armament. Admiral Bey was now trapped between Burnett's cruisers to the north and Fraser's warships to the south, and he had no choice but to fight it out. Once the *Scharnhorst*'s gunners had recovered from their surprise, their fire was accurate, but although they straddled the British battleship many times, they failed to register a serious hit on her. The *Duke of York*'s gunnery was excellent; she scored 31 straddles out of 52 broadsides, with enough hits to put the battlecruiser's 'A' and 'B' turrets out of action and to rupture some steam pipes, which reduced her speed so that Bey had no chance of out-running his adversaries, even if given the opportunity.

At 1824 hours, the third of the *Scharnhorst*'s turrets was put out of action. Fraser realized that the *Duke of York*'s 35.5cm (14in) shells, when fired at short range with a flat trajectory, were unlikely to pierce the enemy's armour, so he turned away to let the destroyers finish the job. Two of them, the *Savage* and *Saumarez*, approached from the north-west under heavy fire, firing starshell, while the *Scorpion* and *Stord* attacked fom the south-east, launching their torpedoes at 1849. As Hintze turned his ship to port to engage them, one of the *Scorpio*'s torpedoes struck home, closely followed by three more from the first two destroyers. As the small ships retired under cover of smoke, the *Duke of York* and the cruisers closed in to batter the enemy warship with merciless fire. As Lieutenant B.B. Ramsden, an officer of Royal Marines on HMS *Jamaica*, later wrote, the Scharnhorst 'must have been a hell on earth. The 14-inch shells from the flagship were hitting or rocketing off from a ricochet on the sea. Great flashes rent the night, and the sound of gunfire was continuous, and yet she replied, but only occasionally now with what armament she had left.'

FREEZING SEAS

By 1930 hours, the battlecruiser was a blazing wreck, her hull glowing red-hot in the Arctic night, and the destroyers closed in to finish her off with torpedoes. At 1945 hours, she

Right: The *Tirpitz* photographed by a PRU Spitfire in Kaafjord. Reconnaissance Spitfires flew to airfields in northern Russia to carry out such missions, which were vital to the safety of Allied convoys.

blew up, and only 36 of her crew of 1968 officers and men were rescued from the freezing seas. Like their comrades of the *Bismarck* two and a half years earlier, they had fought their ship gallantly to the end; now, treated with great kindness by the destroyer men who pulled them from the oil-soaked water, they were transferred to the *Duke of York* for the voyage to England, and captivity.

So ended the Battle of North Cape, and with it the last attempt by a German capital ship to challenge the supremacy of the Royal Navy.

The *Tirpitz*, meanwhile, had retreated to Kaafjord, a narrow body of water leading off Altenfjord, to undergo repairs. The berth had been selected earlier, as the high, steep mountains on both sides of the fjord made air attack very difficult, especially for torpedo-bombers. On the night of 10–11 February 1944, however, 15 Ilyushin Il-4 bombers of the Soviet Naval Air Arm, each carrying a 1000kg (2250lb) bomb, set out to attack the battleship. Four of the Soviet crews found their target, and one bomb registered a near miss, causing slight damage.

In a bid to knock the *Tirpitz* out once and for all, before she could be made fully seaworthy again, the C-in-C Home Fleet (now Admiral Sir Bruce Fraser) planned a massive Fleet Air Arm strike against her. To simulate her anchorage in Altenfjord, a dummy range was built on Loch Eriboll, in Caithness, Scotland, and during March 1944 this was the scheme of intense activity as aircraft from the *Victorious* and *Furious* rehearsed the attack plan.

AIR STRIKE

The strike was to be carried out by the 8th and 52nd TBR (Torpedo Bomber Reconnaissance) Wings, operating the Fairey Barracuda, a type that had first seen action during the Salerno landings in Italy eight months earlier. In addition to their TBR Wings, the *Victorious* and *Furious* also carried Nos 1834 and 1836 Squadrons, equipped with American-built Vought Corsair fighters, and Nos. 801 and 880 Squadrons with Seafires. More fighter cover was to be provided by the Hellcats of Nos. 800 and 804 Squadrons (carried by HMS *Emperor*) and the Martlet Vs of Nos. 861, 896, 882 and 898 Squadrons (carried by HMS *Pursuer* and *Searcher*), while anti-submarine patrols were to be flown by the Swordfish of 842 Squadron on board HMS *Fencer*. The carrier group was

to be covered by warships of the Home Fleet, consisting of the battleships *Duke of York* and *Anson*, the cruisers *Belfast*, *Jamaica*, *Royalist* and *Sheffield* and 14 destroyers, and the strike was timed to coincide with the passage of a Russian convoy, JW58.

On 30 March 1944, with the convoy well on its way, the Home Fleet units sailed from Scapa Flow in two forces, the first comprising the two battleships, the *Victorious*, one cruiser and five destroyers, and the second comprising the *Furious*, the four escort carriers and three cruisers. The actual attack on the *Tirpitz*, code-named Operation Tungsten, was to be conducted by Vice-Admiral Sir Henry Moore, second-in-command of the Home Fleet, flying his flag in the *Anson*.

The forces assembled on the afternoon of 2 April about 350km (220nm) to the north-west of Altenfjord and from there moved to the flying-off position, 222km (120nm) north-west of Kaafjord, reaching it during the early hours of the following morning. At 0430 hours, 21 Barracudas of No. 8 TBR Wing, escorted by 21 Corsairs and 20 Hellcats, took off from the *Victorious* and set course for the target. Eighty km (50 miles) from their objective, the Barracudas, which had been flying low over the sea to avoid radar detection, went up to 2440m (8000ft) and began their final approach, preceded by the fighters, which went in at low level to suppress flak. The Germans were taken by surprise and the *Tirpitz*, lying virtually naked under the beginnings of a smoke screen, was hit by nine armour-piercing or semi-armour-piercing bombs.

An hour later, a second attack was made by 19 Barracudas of No. 52 TBR Wing, escorted by 39 fighters, and the performance was repeated. By this time the smoke screen was fully developed, but it hindered the German gunners far more than it did the Barracuda crews, who had no difficulty in locating their target.

In all, the battleship was hit by 14 bombs, 122 of her crew being killed and 316 wounded; although the bombs failed to penetrate her heavy armour, they caused extensive damage to her superstructure and fire control systems and put her out of action for a further three months. The British lost two Barracudas and a Hellcat.

ENEMY CONVOYS

Further attempts to attack the *Tirpitz* in May were frustrated by bad weather, the naval aircraft instead turning their attention to enemy convoys off the Norwegian coast and scoring some successes. It was not until 17 July 1944 that another raid was carried out, this time by aircraft from the *Formidable*, *Furious* and *Indefatigable* under the command of Rear-Admiral R.R. McGrigor. The covering force, comprising the battleship *Duke of York*, the cruisers *Bellona*, *Devonshire*, *Jamaica* and *Kent*, was commanded by Admiral Sir Henry Moore, now Commander-in-Chief Home Fleet in place of Admiral Sir Bruce Fraser. Forty-five Barracudas of Nos. 820 and 826 Squadrons (*Indefatigable*) and 827 and 830 Squadrons (*Formidable*) set out to make the attack; the 50-strong fighter escort included the Fairey Fireflies of No.

1770 Squadron, making their appearance in combat for the first time. However, the enemy had plenty of warning on this occasion. The smoke screen obscured the warship, the AA defences were fully alerted, and the raid was unsuccessful.

The next attack, carried out on 22 August, was a disaster: the incoming aircraft were detected a long way from the target and were intercepted by Me 109s of JG5, the Luftwaffe's 'Arctic Wing', which shot down 11 of them, mostly Barracudas. The escort carrier *Nabob* was torpedoed off North Cape by the *U534* and damaged beyond repair; the *U534* was herself sunk by aircraft from the escort carrier Vindex three days later. Two minor bomb hits were obtained on the *Tirpitz* in an attack on 24 August, the Barracuda crews bombing blind through the smoke, and a further attack, on the 29th, was unsuccessful. Counting a mission that had to be aborted because of the weather on 20 August, the Fleet Air Arm flew 247 sorties in this series of attacks.

HIGHBALL

For a long time, the RAF had been formulating plans of its own to attack the *Tirpitz* and other heavy German surface

Below: The Fleet Air Arm's bombs bursting on and around the *Tirpitz* during the attack of 3 April 1944. This raid (Operation Tungsten) clearly showed the effectiveness of dive bombers.

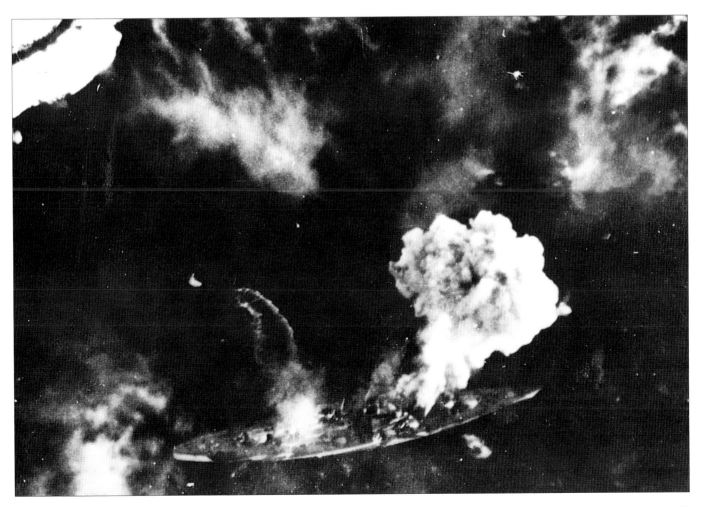

Above: The cruiser HMS *Kent* was one of the warships assigned to protect the aircraft carriers that launched air strikes against the *Tirpitz*. She survived the war and was scrapped in 1948.

units in Norway, using a special weapon code-named Highball. A spherical weapon, designed to be carried by the de Havilland Mosquito, Highball worked on the same principle as the Wallis mine, the weapon developed to breach the Ruhr Dams. Spinning backwards at up to 1000rpm after release, Highball bounced across the water until striking its target. After rebounding, it spun forwards again under the ship, where it was exploded by means of a hydrostatic fuze. A 272kg (600lb) explosive charge was contained in Highball, and the Mosquito could carry two of these weapons in tandem in its bomb bay, with the doors removed.

Work on Highball, including dropping trials, was undertaken by Vickers in April 1943; a special Coastal Command unit, No. 618 Squadron, had been formed on the 1st of that month. For the first two weeks of its existence, No. 618 Squadron used standard Mosquito Mk IV bombers; the first converted aircraft arrived at Skitten, the squadron's base in northern Scotland, on 18 April. Another five arrived by the end of the month. The Highball programme eventually involved 60 Mosquito IVs, but 30 of these were subsequently reconverted to carry an 1812kg (4000lb) bomb.

PLANNED ATTACK

No. 618 Squadron began dropping trials with Highball on 13 April 1943, three days before the first of the larger spinning mines (code-named Upkeep) was dropped from a Lancaster. Between then and the end of the month, 23 drops were made, using prototype weapons and the Reculver reservoir. At the same time, the squadron's crews were training in long-distance navigation, and in attacks on shipping from high and low level. Much of this practice was against a target vessel, the *Bonaventura*, in Loch Cairnbairn. The original plan was for No. 618 Squadron to attack the *Tirpitz* with Highball and No. 617 Squadron to attack the Ruhr dams

with Upkeep on consecutive nights in May. This would have been a spectacular double coup, but the possibility of it vanished when difficulties were encountered with Highball's behaviour. Following trials against armoured targets, a new bomb casing was developed. In May, the squadron operated from Turnberry and Manston, dropping Highballs from a height of 15.2–18.3m (50–60ft) with a ground speed of 587km/h (360mph). The weapon was spun at 700rpm and a range of 1097m (1200 yards) was achieved, but persistent problems were experienced with the release mechanism. In one series of ten drops, five Highballs were lost because of this defect. In the end, No. 618 Squadron was grounded in September 1943 and its aircraft and personnel dispersed while Vickers grappled with the problems.

MAJOR SUCCESS

Dropping trials with a new batch of improved weapons began in December 1943 against target vessels in Loch Striven. These were interrupted when the squadron's crews were diverted to take part in conventional shipping strikes, using 'borrowed' Mosquitoes, but in May 1944 the first major success was achieved. During this month, some 50 drops were made, including the first double drop from a single aircraft, and a target ship was holed for the first time. Work continued throughout the summer of 1944, and in September No. 618 Squadron completed its dropping trials over Loch Striven with the fully developed Highball. This achieved a range of 488m (1600ft) when dropped from 15.2m (50ft) at 587km/h (365mph), rotating at up to 1000rpm. The weapon had a total weight of 567kg (1250lb).

By this time, however, it had been decided to deploy No. 618 Squadron to the Pacific for operations against the Japanese, and at the end of October the squadron left for Australia aboard the escort carriers HMS *Striker* and *Fencer*. The Highballs, now known popularly as 'Johnnie Walkers', were never used operationally, mainly because the British and Americans could not agree on how best to integrate No. 618 Squadron into the Pacific scheme of things. The squadron disbanded in June 1945 and its Highballs were destroyed.

TALLBOY BOMBS

An attack on the *Tirpitz* with Highball, at night and at low level, might conceivably have worked, provided No. 618 Squadron could have achieved the necessary element of surprise; the Mosquitoes were fast enough to make their approach before the *Tirpitz*'s defences could be fully activated, and agile enough to clear the fjord's natural obstacles. By the summer of 1944, however, the RAF had another formidable weapon, and one moreover that might be used to attack the battleship with much less attendant risk. Known as Tallboy, it was a 5443kg (12,000lb) deep-penetration bomb, also designed by Barnes Wallis. A remarkable weapon, it had the explosive power of a high-capacity blast bomb and the penetrating power of an armour-piercing bomb without sacrificing explosive filling for thickness of casing. Its secret lay in its perfect streamlining, which gave it a terminal velocity of 1098m/sec (3600ft/sec). Its use required a high degree of accuracy, because in order to achieve maximum penetration it had to be dropped from a height of 2440m (8000ft) or more.

The Tallboy was pioneered into service by No. 617 Squadron, which, since its successful attack on the Ruhr

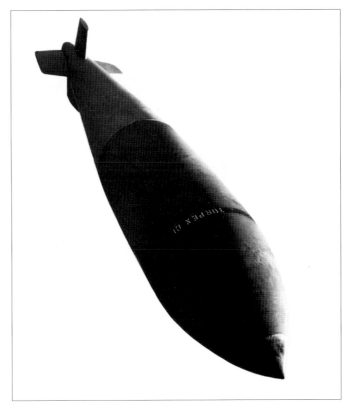

Above: The six-ton Tallboy bomb that sent the Tirpitz to her doom. Developed by Dr Barnes Wallis, who also devised the special weapons that destroyed the Ruhr Dams, the Tallboy was also effective against U-boat pens.

dams in May 1943, had fulfilled the role of Bomber Command's operational trials unit. The squadron's specially modified Lancasters were fitted with new Mk IIA bomb sights, which enabled their crews to place the bombs within 75m (250ft) of the target from an altitude of 6100m (20,000ft). This margin of error was quite unacceptable, for the exploding Tallboy displaced $764600m^3$ (1 million ft^3) of earth and formed a crater that took 5081 tonnes (5000 tons) of soil to fill.

HARD TARGETS

No. 617 Squadron's first Tallboy mission was carried out on the night of 8–9 June 1944, when it destroyed the Saumur railway tunnel in southern France, a vital point on the main rail artery through which the Germans

Left: Armourers loading 226kg (500lb) bombs on to the wing racks of a de Havilland Mosquito. The spherical Highball bomb required modifications to the Mosquito's bomb bay.

were bringing reinforcements from the south-west to the Normandy front. During the weeks that followed, the squadron's Tallboy-armed Lancasters hit more 'hard' targets, notably the U-boat pens at Brest, Lorient, St Nazaire and La Pallice, and the S-boat bases at Le Havre and Boulogne, all of which were protected by thick concrete. Then they struck, by day, at the V-1 construction sites at Siracourt, Watten, Wizernes and Mimoyeques. In September 1944, they breached the Dortmund-Ems canal, and in October they destroyed the Kembs Dam, on the upper Rhine north of Basle. By the late summer of 1944, therefore, No. 617 Squadron's crews were very experienced in the use of Tallboys, and a second Lancaster squadron, No. 9, had also been converted to drop the huge bombs. The squadrons were based, respectively, at Woodhall Spa and Bardney, in Lincolnshire.

In August 1944, and on the orders of HQ Bomber Command, No. 5 Group (to which No 617 Squadron belonged), had begun to assess the feasibility of using the Tallboy to destroy the *Tirpitz*. It was the only bomb in existence capable of penetrating the battleship's two layers of deck armour, the upper layer being 100mm (3.93in) and the lower one 120mm (4.7in) thick.

Above: Fairey Barracuda dive-bombers en route to attack the *Tirpitz*. The Barracuda was not a popular aircraft, but it was effective in the dive-bombing role. It was also used as a torpedo-bomber.

APPALLING WEATHER

Range was a principal problem; Kaafjord lay 2224km (1200nm) from the nearest British airfield, beyond the capability of the Lancaster bombers that carried the Tallboy. To overcome this, agreement was reached with the Russians that the Lancasters of Nos. 9 and 617 Squadrons – the specialist 'Tallboy' squadrons – would strike at the *Tirpitz* from the Soviet airfield of Yagodnik, on the Archangel peninsula. After a great deal of planning and organisation, 38 Lancasters of the two squadrons set out for North Russia in the evening of 11 September 1944. Of this force, which encountered appalling weather en route, one aircraft aborted and returned to Britain when its Tallboy bomb broke loose and had to be jettisoned, six more crash-landed in Russia and had to be abandoned, and two were immediately judged unfit for operations on arrival at Yagodnik. Two Liberators carrying the ground crews arrived safely, as did a weather reconnaissance Mosquito and a Lancaster carrying an RAF film unit.

THE *TIRPITZ* DATA AT A GLANCE			
Displacement	42,900t standard; 52,600t full load		main turrets 362mm–178mm
Dimensions	248 x 36 x 10.6m (813ft 8in x 118ft		(14.25in–7in); secondary turrets
	1in x 34ft 9in)		102mm–37mm (4in–1.5in); conning
Machinery	three-shaft Brown-Boveri geared		tower 356mm (14in)
	turbines, 138,000hp 110,000hp	Armament	eight 38cm (15in); 12 15cm (5.9in);
Max speed	29 knots		16 105mm (4.1in); 16 37mm; 12
Range	15,750km (8500nm) at 19 knots		(later 58) 20mm; eight 533mm (21in) TT
Armour	belt 318mm–267mm (1.25–1.05in);	Complement	2092
	deck 121mm–51mm (4.75in–2in);		

On 15 September, 27 Lancasters, plus the film unit aircraft, took off from Yagodnik to attack the battleship. No problem was envisaged with the weather, for the reconnaissance Mosquito had surveyed the bombers' route earlier and had reported that conditions were favourable. The main obstacle to the success of the mission was likely to be the massive defensive smokescreen that the Germans were known to be capable of laying across the *Tirpitz*'s anchorage (though for a very short time).

TWO WAVES

The plan called for the bombers to attack in two waves. The first, consisting of 21 Lancasters carrying Tallboys, was to bomb from between 4270 and 5490m (14,000 and 18,000ft), while behind them at between 3050 and 6660m (10,000 and 12,000ft) came six more Lancasters carrying 225kg (500lb) mines, which were smaller versions of the Highball and specially developed for attacking vessels moored in shallow water. Initially the whole force was to make its approach at 300m (1000ft) to achieve the maximum element of surprise. This height was to be maintained until the Finnish border was reached, when the bombers were to climb to between 610 and 915m (2000 and 3000ft) above their bombing height. This would enable them to make their bombing run in a shallow dive, affording the extra speed that would be vital if the bombs were to be released before the enemy smokescreen had time to form.

BLANKET OF SMOKE

As they approached, the Tallboy-armed Lancasters strayed off track, their compasses having been made unreliable by the large iron ore deposits in the mountains. This necessitated a major course alteration, but apart from this, the flight to the target was uneventful. As they approached the fjord in an almost cloudless sky, the crews had a clear view of the battleship. Then the smokescreen began to form and she was quickly obscured, but five Tallboys went down in her immediate vicinity during the next 60 seconds. The crews that followed took the battleship's flak bursts as their aiming point, and some felt sure that more than one hit had been obtained. There was, however, no way of obtaining any confirmation at this stage, for as the Lancasters left the target area the whole fjord lay under a dense blanket of smoke. Post-raid reconnaissance was also frustrated by cloud, which began to creep across the sky soon after the attack, and when the reconnaissance Mosquito arrived over Altenfjord some two hours later, its crew got only a brief glimpse of the vessel through a gap.

In fact, the *Tirpitz* had been damaged to a far greater extent than any of the attacking crews dreamed. One Tallboy had gone straight through her overhanging bow and exploded in the water, the force of the explosion wrecking the deck plating as far as the forward turret and causing further damage to her main engine frames. It was estimated

Above: On 15 September 1944, the *Tirpitz* was further damaged by Tallboys dropped by 27 Lancasters that attacked her from a base in North Russia. The battleship is hidden by smoke, top right.

that even if she could reach a north German shipyard with full repair facilities, it would be at least nine months before she could be made battleworthy again. The Germans, however, declined to risk the battleship in a slow voyage down the Norwegian coast; at 6 or 7 knots, the best speed she could make with her damaged engines, she would be a sitting target. Instead, they sent her to a new anchorage at Tromsö, from where it was planned that her heavy armament would help repel an Allied invasion of northern Norway. She was protected from underwater attack by a double net barrage, and from air attack by smokescreens, anti-aircraft batteries on the shore and two flak ships, Nymph and Thetis.

STILL AFLOAT

The British Admiralty had at this stage no way of knowing that the *Tirpitz*'s fighting days were over. As far as Naval Intelligence was concerned, Tromsö might simply be a staging point for some other destination. At any rate, the warship was still afloat and therefore continued to present a threat. By 24 October another plan had been devised for an

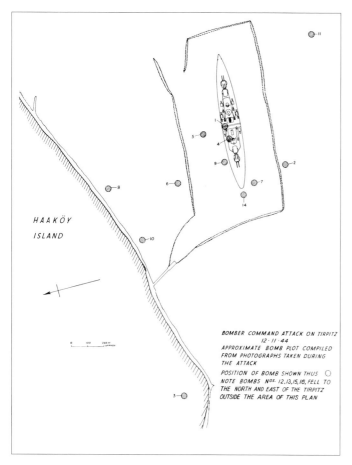

HAAKÖY
ISLAND

BOMBER COMMAND ATTACK ON TIRPITZ
12·11·44
APPROXIMATE BOMB PLOT COMPILED
FROM PHOTOGRAPHS TAKEN DURING
THE ATTACK
POSITION OF BOMB SHOWN THUS ○
NOTE BOMBS NOS. 12,13,15,16, FELL TO
THE NORTH AND EAST OF THE TIRPITZ
OUTSIDE THE AREA OF THIS PLAN

Left: This diagram shows where the Tallboy bombs fell during the RAF attack on 12 November 1944. The *Tirpitz* received two direct hits by the armour-piercing bombs, enough to destroy her.

the attack phase was to be flown at 610m (2000ft) the oxygen would not be missed. Even with all these weight-saving precautions, the bombers' fuel capacity would be minimal, and pilots were told that any Lancaster with less than 4,090 litres (900 gallons) remaining after the attack was to carry on to Russia and land at Yagodnik or Vaenga.

HEAVY FLAK

On the morning of 20 October, the strike force was ready. It consisted of 18 Lancasters of No. 617 Squadron and 18 of No. 9, led respectively by Wing Commanders J.B. Tait and J.M. Bazin. The aircraft took off in pouring rain and reached the target area at 0900 hours. The crews had a clear view of the *Tirpitz* as they began their run-in, but at the very last moment – 30 seconds before the first Lancaster was ready to bomb – low cloud drifted in from the sea and obscured the anchorage. Thirty-three aircraft attacked through heavy flak and dropped their Tallboys, aiming through partial gaps in the cloud, but they were able to claim only one near miss. One aircraft was damaged by flak and force-landed in Sweden.

For twelve days, the two squadrons stood by, waiting for a favourable opportunity to strike at the battleship once more. At 0200 hours on 12 November 1944, 30 Lancasters again set out from Lossiemouth, making landfall on the Norwegian close in brilliantly clear weather. At a distance of 32km (20 miles), the crews sighted the *Tirpitz*. There was no cloud, no

attack on the battleship in her new anchorage, and Nos. 9 and 617 Squadrons were once more working out the details of the operation.

This time, since Tromsö was some 370km (200nm) closer to the British Isles than Altenfjord, it was decided to launch the attack from a home base: Lossiemouth, in Scotland. The round trip involved a flight of 4170km (2250nm), so to compensate for the weight of the Tallboys and the extra fuel required the Lancasters were stripped of all equipment that was not considered absolutely necessary. The front guns, mid-upper gun turrets, ammunition, oxygen bottles and armour plating were all removed. Since no enemy fighters had been encountered during the previous attack, the elimination of most of the Lancasters' firepower seemed a justifiable risk, and as all the flight with the exception of

Right: The whole attack on the *Tirpitz* was filmed by a Film Unit crew on board a Lancaster. This 'still' shows smoke billowing from the stricken battleship, while another bomb explodes on the shore.

smokescreen. Like a great spider nestling in a web of anti-submarine booms, the battleship lay naked.

The *Tirpitz* opened fire, and soon she was obscured by the smoke of her armament. The Lancasters continued their bombing runs through countless shellbursts flung up by the battleship, the two flak ships and the shore batteries, and at 0940 hours Wng Cdr Tait released the first Tallboy. More bombs went down as Tait dived away to port, exploding on or around the battleship, raising immense columns of smoke and water. As Tait and his crew watched, a column of steam shot up to a height of 100m (330ft), penetrating the darker clouds of smoke that shrouded the warship.

TORN APART

Following the main force came a Lancaster of No. 463 Squadron, filming the attack. As it ran overhead, its crew saw the battleship slowly capsize, torn apart by two direct hits and a massive internal explosion. When a Mosquito photographed the scene two hours later, the *Tirpitz* had almost completely turned turtle in the shallow waters of the fjord, her superstructure resting on the bottom.

Above: Allied personnel examine one of the *Tirpitz*'s massive propeller shafts. The process of cutting up the battleship went on for years. Some 900 crew members and civilians perished in the attack.

Twenty-eight officers, including the *Tirpitz*'s latest commander, Captain Weber, and 874 crewmen perished with the ship; 880 were rescued. The cost to the RAF was one Lancaster, which came down in Sweden with flak damage, its crew unharmed.

The remains of the *Tirpitz*, with the bodies of many of her crew still trapped inside, lay in her last resting place for a dozen years, being cut up slowly piece by piece, her rusting hulk a testament to Nazi Germany's vain hopes of gaining dominion of the seas. Yet in the annals of naval history, *Tirpitz* and her sister ship the *Bismarck*, would forever remain symbols of magnificent battleship construction. It was not any fault of the ships, or of their crews, that had led to the failure of their respective missions. The fault lay with the muddled planning and strategy, the lack of perception and foresight which, ultimately, was to lead to the downfall of the Third Reich itself.

CHAPTER 5

The *Bismarck* Revisited

The fascination with the battleship *Bismarck* persisted for decades after she met her end, and the discovery of her wreck has led to an upsurge of interest.

In July 1988, the explorer and scientist Dr Robert D. Ballard, who had earned considerable fame and prestige by locating the wreck of the ill-fated liner RMS *Titanic* in 1985, launched an expedition to locate the sunken *Bismarck*. During a second expedition to the *Titanic*, the remains of the liner had been thoroughly explored with the aid of a deep-submersible robot called Jason; Ballard now planned to use a similar technique to locate and survey the *Bismarck*, this time with the aid of a more advanced two-ton underwater robot named Argo. One of the expedition's main backers was the Quest Group, a company formed by two American businessmen.

The base for the expediton was a deep-sea trawler, the *Starella*, chartered from the English east coast port of Hull. Having carried out some survey work in the Mediterranean, the expedition sailed from La Coruna, Spain, and reached the presumed site of the *Bismarck* wreck, 965km (600 miles) west of Brest, on 11 July 1988. The outward voyage was dogged by bad weather, which showed no signs of clearing when the expedition reached the site. The team's first action was to deploy three transponders, acoustic beacons that enabled Argo to navigate its way across the ocean floor with pinpoint accuracy. The Argo communicated with these transponders, which in turn communicated with a small torpedo-shaped device, known as the pollywog, towed astern of the ship. The information was instantly processed by computer and the information displayed on a console in the control centre on the vessel. Argo was designed to be towed by a cable through which commands were passed to it by its 'pilot' in the control centre. This was a tricky task, as the vehicle had to be towed close to the ocean floor so that its video cameras could register debris. In this case, Argo also had to negotiate an underwater mountain on which two of the

Left: The bridge area of the *Bismarck*, showing the mount for the forward rangefinder. Manoeuvring the robot explorer over the ocean floor with pinpoint accuracy was a tricky task.

Above: The Ocean Explorer 6000 side-scan sonar was used to locate the *Bismarck* and the *Hood* on an expedition mounted in 2000 by Blue Water Recoveries, led by the explorer David Mearns.

transponders had landed. Further problems were caused by the equipment on board the Starella: there was trouble, for example, with the winch that paid out and reeled in Argo's 6060m (20,000ft) coaxial cable.

All these problems were compounded by uncertainty over the actual wreck site, since the sinking reports logged by the British warships that had sent *Bismarck* to the bottom were conflicting. To cover the whole area would mean surveying 520km² (200 miles²) of ocean bed, which was simply not feasible in the prevailing conditions, with equipment that was in danger of failing and in stormy conditions.

FALSE ALARMS

For several days, the *Starella* tracked back and forth, the sonar search over an area 48km (30 miles) square punctuated by occasional false alarms caused mostly by natural geological features that were mistaken for disturbances on the sea bed denoting where a large vessel might have impacted. Then came what the crew fervently hoped was the breakthrough, when the Argo picked up some fragments of what appeared to be debris, followed by an impact crater. The area was only about a nautical mile southeast of the sinking of the *Bismarck*, as estimated in the log of the battleship HMS *Rodney*. Dr Ballard and his colleagues spent hours trying to identify the debris from the images transmitted back by the

Argo, and to match them with known parts of the *Bismarck*'s superstructure. But where was the ship itself? Several theories were put forward, foremost among them being that the debris consisted of pieces blasted from the battleship by British gunfire while she was still afloat. The main body of the wreck might still be a considerable distance away. But what about the impact crater? Was it possible that this really was the last resting place of the *Bismarck*, and that the mightly battleship had buried herself completely in the soft mud of the ocean bed? It seemed unlikely, but Ballard decided that no further clues were likely to emerge until he had had an opportunity to carry out a thorough analysis of the photographs taken by Argo's still camera, which would be crisper than the video footage.

On 21 July, a week after the first debris and the impact crater had been discovered, the search was abandoned. A few days after that, having examined hundreds of colour slides from Argo's camera, Ballard knew the truth. Among the fragmented wreckage, the camera had picked out a larger artefact that was quickly identified as a wooden rudder. Other pieces proved to be the remains of a bilge pump, deadeyes for sails, and pieces of copper lining that clearly had once been attached to a wooden hull. What Argo had discovered was the remains of a four-masted sailing schooner, probably of late 19th-century vintage. For the time being, Ballard had no choice but to leave *Bismarck* with her secrets intact.

SECOND EXPEDITION

On 25 May 1989, having secured the necesary funding, Dr Ballard launched a second expedition from Cadiz, Spain, this time having the benefit of a much sounder vessel. She was the oil rig support ship *Star Hecules*, normally based at Aberdeen in Scotland. Earlier in May, fitted out as a sophisticated command centre, she had toured the Mediterranean, broadcasting live TV programmes on underwater geology and archaeology to schoolchildren in the United States.

This time, the weather was favourable, with fine and sunny conditions prevailing throughout the three-day voyage to the search area. This was reached on 29 May, and after fixing the ship's exact location with the aid of the Global Positioning System (GPS), the crew deployed the sonar equipment. They lowered Argo to its operating depth of about 5km (3 miles), only to find when its systems were checked that two of its three cameras were not working. There was no alternative but to raise the submersible for repairs, and it was not until the following day that the search operation could begin.

MOUNTAINOUS AREA

Dr Ballard had decided to carry out the search in a series of east–west lines spaced about a mile apart, the first running between the recorded positions of HMS *Dorsetshire* to the north and *King George V* to the south, his starting point being inside the search area covered in the previous year at a spot in what is known as the Porcupine Abyssal Plain. The track followed by Argo would have to cross a mountainous area rising to some 3000m (1000ft), which Ballard had been at pains to avoid on the earlier expedition. In fact, it was the site of an extinct volcano, about 16km (10 miles) across, and it proved relatively easy to negotiate. However, although a few isolated pieces of nondescript debris were sighted, there was nothing to suggest a wreckage trail, even after the search had been in progress for nearly a week and around 80 per cent of the search area covered.

Then, at midnight on 5 June 1989, the questing lights of the Argo picked up the beginnings of a debris field – the trail of as yet unidentifiable objects – orientated south–north. Soon afterwards, the submersible discovered what appeared to be a huge landslide, running south-east to north-west. Ballard reasoned that if the impact of the *Bismarck* had caused the

Below: Further proof of *Bismarck*'s durability: this photograph shows damage caused by a shell that failed to penetrate her hull. The battleship had no fewer than 22 watertight compartments.

landslide, the bulk of the wreck must lie where the path of the landslide and the wreckage trail intersected. He was right. As Argo continued to probe its way across the ocean floor, it came upon what seemed to be clear evidence of an impact crater, large pieces of wreckage, and the chilling sight of a sea-man's boot, lying on the sediment. More boots, a great many of them, were sighted later, as Argo followed the landslide.

SONAR TARGET

It was late on 6 June that a solitary gun turret was discovered, lying upside down in the sediment. But there was no sign of the remainder of the ship; a day-long search on 7 June revealed nothing apart from more chunks of wreckage, including part of the superstructure complete with portholes. On the tenth day of the search, 8 June, a large sonar target was reported 200m (50ft) to starboard of the submersible. Despite its prox-imity, it took a long time to circle and home Argo on to the contact; manoeuvring a submersible at the end of a 5km (3 mile) cable is no easy task. Then, jutting from what looked like a steep slope, Ballard and his colleagues saw two gun barrels, protruding from a turret, and realized that they were looking at part of the *Bismarck*'s 15cm (5.9in) secondary armament.

Above: One of the first images to be detected by Argo's underwater camera, looming out of the freezing darkness of 5km (3 miles) down, was this twin gun turret, still filled with menace.

In fact it was the starboard middle turret, and shortly after-wards the cameras zoomed in on a second turret, the star-board 10.5cm (4.12in) anti-aircraft position. This turret was badly damaged, its guns askew.

Bismarck's hull was upright on the seabed, and as Argo's robot cameras began their survey of her upperworks, it became clear what had happened during the battleship's final plunge. In the dying moments of the battle, she had slowly begun to sink by the stern, and just before sinking she had rolled over, her bow clear of the water. The four main gun turrets and other heavy debris broke clear and began their descent, as did the extreme stern, weakened by the tor-pedo that had jammed the rudders. Fully flooded, the *Bismarck* too began her descent; with all air expelled, she quickly righted herself and picked up speed as the descent continued. Ten to 20 minutes after leaving the surface, her hull impacted halfway up the slope of the underwater vol-cano, setting off a massive landslide. The main turrets, which

impacted just before the hull, were swept along with the deluge of mud and silt. The whole ensemble – hull, turrets and other heavy pieces of wreckage – continued down the slope, leaving huge scars as they went, before coming to rest about two-thirds of the way down the mountainside. For hours afterwards, lighter wreckage continued to drift down, forming the debris field.

LAST BATTLE

Argo continued to survey the wreck for five hours, sending back video images and taking photographs the whole time. What they revealed astonished the observers, not so much by the amount of punishment the *Bismarck* had taken during her last battle, but by how intact the great warship was. Although all four main turrets were missing, the secondary armament was still intact and the mountings of the anti-aircraft guns were still in place, although some of the barrels were missing. The forward superstructure had been blasted away, and there were more than 50 shell holes around the area of the conning tower, which itself showed little evidence of damage. There was much evidence, however, of direct hits from heavy-calibre shells, especially HMS

Above: A commemorative plaque, bearing the names of all those who died recorded on a CD, was laid on the wreckage of the *Bismarck's* superstructure in July 2001. A similar plaque was laid on HMS *Hood*.

Rodney's 40.6cm (16in) monsters, but in this case the damage toll had not been entirely one-sided. One of the *Bismarck's* last salvoes had near-missed the British battleship and jammed her port torpedo tube doors. But the greatest damage to the *Rodney* had been caused by the almost continuous firing of her own main armament, the concussion of which had ruptured tile decking in washrooms and lavatories throughout the ship, as well as breaking or cracking many longitudinal beams. Overhead decking was also ruptured and many bolts and rivets sheared, causing serious leaks. Every compartment on the main deck experienced flooding, this being caused mostly by the rupturing of cast iron water mains. Bulkheads, furniture, lockers and fittings broke loose, causing further damage as the ship rolled.

EERIE SIGHT

Argo's cameras also revealed something Ballard and his colleagues had not expected to see: the eerie sight of the

swastikas, painted on the deck near stem and stern for air-craft recognition purposes. After all this time in the deep, the paintwork was still preserved.

With darkness approaching and the weather deteriorating, Dr Ballard ordered Argo to be raised. The submersible emerged entangled in fishing net, lost or cut loose by some unknown deep-sea trawler. A second exploration was made the next day, 9 June, and this confirmed that the *Bismarck* had sustained the worst damage on her port side, which had come under the heaviest fire from *Rodney* and *King George V*. The second survey also revealed more damage caused by the secondary armament of the British warships, although Bismarck's armour had been well capable of withstanding most hits from lesser-calibre guns. A third attempted survey, on 11 June, ended in failure when Argo was damaged as it approached the barbette where the aftermost turret, Dora, had once been seated. That evening, a wreath fashioned out of rope was dropped overboard near the *Bismarck*'s final resting place – 965km (600 miles) west of Brest and 611km (380 miles) south of Cork, Ireland, at a depth of 4790m (15,700ft). *Star Hecules* and her crew then set course for a port in southern England.

Above: A side view of the mighty *Bismarck*, illustrating her sleek lines and 'clipper' bow. She and *Tirpitz* represented the apex of German warship design.

CONTROVERSY

The discovery of the *Bismarck*, and the resulting photographic evidence, reopened a controversy that has raged ever since that last battle in May 1941. Was the mighty battleship really sunk by British gunfire and torpedoes, or was she scuttled by her own crew? The available evidence seems to point towards the latter, as there was no sign of the implosions that occur when an air-filled compartment succumbs to the outside pressure of the water – a pressure that would have increased dramatically with every fathom of the *Bismarck*'s final descent. At 5km (3 miles) down, the pressure is measured in tons per square inch; no area of unequal pressure, such as an air-filled compartment, could resist that without caving in.

The discovery of the battleship evoked mixed feelings. The Federal German government made its standpoint quite clear in an open statement:

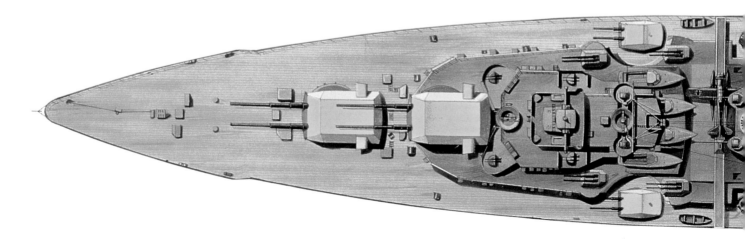

'The Federal Republic of Germany considers itself the owner of the former sovereign battleship *Bismarck*. Diving excursions to the interior of the wreck as well as recovery attempts require the consent of the Federal Government. This has been categorically denied in other cases of sunken ships of the World Wars, as it must be anticipated that the remains of the dead may be found in the wreck. The Federal Republic feels it is its duty to protect the seamen who went to their deaths in the sinking of the ship. Following international custom, we view the wreck of the *Bismarck* as a seaman's grave that must be accorded proper respect.'

REVISITED

The wreck was revisited twice in 2001. On the first expedition, organized by Deep Ocean Expeditions from 5–14 June, a memorial plaque made by Blohm und Voss was placed on

Below: Plan view of the *Bismarck*, showing the dispositions of her main and secondary armament. Note the swastika painted on the bow, an aid to recognition from the air, which when first glimpsed underwater was a startling sight for Dr Ballard and his team.

Bismarck, and dives were made on the site by two submersibles from the Russian scientific research vessel *Akademik Keldysh*, carrying 24 passengers as well as the pilots. The second expedition, in July, was organized by Blue Water Recoveries. It visited both the *Bismarck* and the *Hood* and sailed on the survey ship *Northern Horizon*, both wrecks being filmed by cameras mounted in the remotely operated vehicle (ROV) Magellan 725, connected by cable to the mother ship.

A commemorative plaque, together with a roll of all those who died recorded on to a CD, was delivered to the *Hood* via the ROV and placed in position by Ted Briggs, the last of the *Hood*'s survivors.

The combined death toll of those who sailed to destruction in the *Hood* and *Bismarck* was 3315. A further 902 personnel lost their lives when the Tirpitz was sunk in November 1944, bringing the total number of personnel killed in the three ships to 4217.

By way of comparison, the combined total of British and German dead at, for instance, the Battle of Jutland, on 31 May 1916, was 8648.

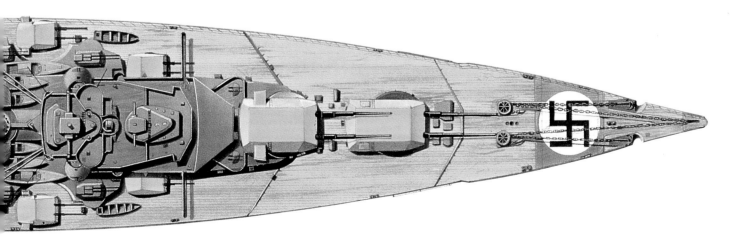

APPENDIX

The Log of the *Bismarck*, 24–27 May 1941: A Chronology of Events

SATURDAY 24 MAY 1941. THE BATTLE OF THE DENMARK STRAIT (KNOWN TO THE GERMANS AS THE ICELAND SEA BATTLE)

0552/0553 hours. Weather: north-east wind force 3–4; sea state 2–3; visibility 15nm; cloud 8/10–10/10. *Hood* and *Prince of Wales* open fire, range 28,900m. *Hood*'s salvo falls between 100m and 300m to port of *Prinz Eugen* (lead ship), bearing 330–340˜; shell splashes approx 30–40m high; *Prinz Eugen* steers through them towards the enemy ships.

0553 hours. *Prince of Wales* opens fire with both forward turrets. Salvo falls about 800/900m short. Cruiser *Suffolk*, 12–15nm astern of *Bismarck*, opens fire; salvoes fall short.

0555–0601 hours. *Prinz Eugen* and *Bismarck* concentrate fire on *Hood*. Incoming salvo from *Prince of Wales*. *Bismarck* is hit on port side by three 35.6cm shells, one in her bows (compartment XXI), and one amidships under the armoured belt (compartment XIV). The third passes through a boat.

0601 hours. *Hood* explodes.

0602–0609 hours. *Bismarck* obtains four hits on *Prince of Wales*, which turns away under cover of smoke. Three hits also obtained by *Prinz Eugen*. *Bismarck* fires last salvo at *Prince of Wales*, bringing total shells expended so far to 93 x 38cm. *Bismarck* is losing oil and has 2000t of water in forecastle. Her top speed is reduced to 28 knots.

0603 hours. *Prinz Eugen* reports torpedo propeller noises to port, bearing 279° and 220°. Unconfirmed. Turns hard to starboard. *Prinz Eugen* has so far expended 183 20.3cm shells.

0632 hours. *Bismarck* reports to Group North: Battleship, probably *Hood*, sunk. Another capital ship, *King George V* or *Renown*, damaged. Two heavy cruisers maintaining contact.

0705 hours. *Bismarck* W/T transmission to Group North: We have sunk a battleship at about 63°10' north, 32°00' west.

0801 hours. *Bismarck* W/T transmission to Group North:

1. Sections XIII–XIV. Electric plant No 4 broken down

2. Port No. 2 boiler room is making water but can be held

3. Maximum speed 28 knots

3. Denmark Strait 50nm wide. Floating mines. Two enemy radar sets recognized

4. Intention: to put in to St Nazaire

Weather, 0900–1200 hours. North-east wind force 2–3. Sea state 3. Visibility 15nm, clear and sunny. Swell from the south. Fog banks from 1100 hours.

1200 hours. Position 60°50' north, 37°50' west.

1240 hours. New course 180°. Speed 24 knots.

1814 hours. *Bismarck* turns 180° to starboard while *Prinz Eugen* leaves formation and proceeds independently.

1840–1856 hours. Fires some shells at *Suffolk* and *Prince of Wales*; no hits.

2056 hours. *Bismarck* W/T transmission to Group West: Shaking off contacts impossible due to enemy radar. Due to fuel (situation), steering to St Nazaire.

2300 hours. *Bismarck* sighted by United States Coast Guard cutter *Modoc*.

SUNDAY 25 MAY 1941. ADMIRAL LÜTJENS' BIRTHDAY

0028 hours. *Bismarck* W/T transmission: Attacked by torpedo aircraft from carrier Victorious. Torpedo hit on starboard side.

0131 hours. *Bismarck* fires two salvoes at *Prince of Wales*. No hits.

0137 hours. *Bismarck* W/T transmission: Expecting further attacks.

0153 hours. *Bismarck* W/T transmission: Torpedo hit of no significance.

0241 hours. Group West W/T transmission: West U-boats have instructions to move east.

0306 hours. Last radar contact by HMS *Suffolk*. No further contact with *Bismarck* for 31 hours. *Bismarck* turns to starboard; new course 130°.

0700 hours. *Bismarck* W/T transmission: One battleship and two heavy cruisers maintaining contact.

0852/1928 hours. *Bismarck* sends 36-minute W/T transmission, which is detected by British wireless intelligence (HF/DF).

0930 hours. British cruiser HMS *Dorsetshire* is diverted from Convoy SL74 to search for *Bismarck*.

1125 hours. W/T transmission from Admiral Raeder to Admiral Lütjens, sending birthday greetings.

MONDAY 26 MAY 1941

1030 hours. *Bismarck* is sighted by Catalina flying boat.

1115 hours. Swordfish aircraft from HMS *Ark Royal* sights *Bismarck*; mistakenly identifies her as a cruiser.

1450/1500 hours. Swordfish torpedo aircraft from *Ark Royal* carry out attack on *Sheffield* in error.

1747 hours. *Sheffield* sights *Bismarck*.

1903 hours. W/T transmission from *Bismarck*: Fuel situation urgent. When can we count on replenishment?

1948 hours. W/T transmission from *U556*. Battleship and *Ark Royal* in sight.

2038 hours. W/T transmission from *U556*. Battleship and aircraft carrier course 115°. High speed.

2055-2125 hours. *Bismarck* is attacked by 15 Swordfish from the carrier *Ark Royal*.

2054 hours. W/T transmission from *Bismarck* to Group West: Attack by carrier aircraft.

2105 hours. W/T transmission from *Bismarck* to Group West: Torpedo hit aft.

2115 hours. W/T transmission from *Bismarck* to Group West: Torpedo hit amidships.

2130-2155 hours. *Bismarck* fires six salvoes at HMS *Sheffield*, range nine miles. No hits.

2140 hours. W/T transmission from *Bismarck* to Group West: Ship unable to manoeuvre. Position approx 47°40'N, 14°50'W. Rudder jammed 15° port.

2238 hours. The Polish destroyer *Piorun* sights *Bismarck* and comes under fire.

2315 hours. Jammed rudders cause *Bismarck* to come round from a southeast to a north-west heading.

2324 hours. *Bismarck* comes under attack by five destroyers (*Cossack*, *Maori*, *Piorun*, *Sikh* and *Zulu*), which are beaten off by heavy fire.

2325 hours. W/T transmission from *Bismarck* to Group West: Surrounded by *Renown* and light forces.

2340 hours. W/T transmission from *Bismarck* to Group West: Ship unmanoeuvrable. We will fight to the last shell. Long live the Führer.

2358 hours. W/T transmission from *Bismarck*: To the Führer of the German Reich Adolf Hitler. We will fight to the last in our trust in you, mein Führer, and in our firm confidence in Germany's victory.

TUESDAY 27 MAY 1941

0153 hours. W/T transmission from Adolf Hitler to Admiral Lütjens and *Bismarck*: I thank you in the name of the whole German Nation – Adolf Hitler. To the crew of battleship *Bismarck*: All Germany is with you. What can now be done will be done. Your devotion to duty will strengthen our people in the struggle for their existence – Adolf Hitler.

0221 hours. W/T transmission from *Bismarck*: Recommend award of the Ritterkreuz to Korvettenkapitän Schneider for sinking the *Hood*.

0351 hours. W/T transmission from German Admiralty to *Bismarck* AO (Artillery Officer) Korvettenkapitän Schneider: The Führer has awarded you

the Ritterkreuz for the sinking of the battleship *Hood*. Heartiest good wishes. Commander-in-Chief Kriegsmarine, Grossadmiral Raeder.

0710 hours. Last W/T transmission from Bismarck to Group West: Send U-boat to take off War Diary.

0800 hours (approx). Weather: wind north-west, 320°, force 6-7; sea state 4-5; visibility 10nm.

0844 hours. *Bismarck* is sighted by the battleships *King George V* and *Rodney* and by the cruisers *Dorsetshire* and *Norfolk*.

0847 hours. HMS *Rodney* opens fire on *Bismarck*.

0849 hours. *Bismarck* opens fire on *Rodney* with forward turrets (Anton and Bruno).

0902 hours. *Bismarck* is hit for the first time; foretop command post disabled.

0908 hours. Forward command post disabled; turrets Anton and Bruno out of action.

0913 hours. Aft command post disabled; turrets Caesar and Dora continue to fire under local control.

0921 hours. Turret Dora put out of action.

0927 hours. One of the forward turrets fires a final salvo.

0931 hours. Turret Caesar fires the last salvo and is put out of action.

0958 hours. *Bismarck* receives a possible torpedo hit on the port side.

1000 hours (approx). Scuttling charges are detonated (according to some crew reports) in the turbine room. All *Bismarck*'s guns are now silent.

1022 hours. After being shelled into a blazing wreck by the British battleships, *Bismarck* is hit in the starboard side by two torpedoes launched by *Dorsetshire* at a range of 3000m (3280 yards).

1037 hours. *Bismarck* is hit on the port side by a third torpedo launched by *Dorsetshire* from 2200m (2400 yards).

1039 hours. *Bismarck* rolls over and sinks in approximate position 48° 10'N, 16°12'W. British warships rescue 115 men.

PRINCIPAL OFFICERS OF THE *BISMARCK*

Captain: Kapitän zur See Ernst Lindemann
First Officer: Fregattenkapitän Hans Oels
Navigation Officer: Korvettenkapitän Wolf Neuendorff
1st Gunnery Officer: Korvettenkapitän Adalbert Schneider
2nd Gunnery Officer: Fregattenkapitän Helmut Albrecht
3rd Gunnery Officer: Korvettenkapitän Burkhard Freiherr von Mullenheim-Rechberg (survivor)
Anti-Aircraft Officer: Kapitänleutnant Karl Gellert
1st Officer of the Watch: Kapitänleutnant Rudolf Troll
Chief Engineer: Korvettenkapitän Dipl-Ing Walter Lehmann
Oberleutnant zur See Jurgen Brandes
Marine-Oberstabsarzt Dr Busch (Medical Officer)
Leutnant zur See Doelker (i/c boarding party)
Dr Externbrink (meteorologist)

Korvettenkapitän Freytag (engineer)
Oberleutnant Giese (engineer)
Leutnant zur See Rolf Hambruch
Kovettenkapitän Hartkopf (disciplinary Officer)
Oberleutnant zur See Friedrich Heuser
Kapitänleutnant Jareis (turbine engineer)
Kapitänleutnant Dipl-Ing Gerhard Junack (damage control officer)
Oberleutnant zur See Kardinal (gunnery control)
Kapitänleutnant Krueger
Oberleutnant zur See Hans-Gerd Lippold
Kapitänleutnant Michatsch
Oberleutnant Richter
Korvettenkapitän Max Rollmann
Marinebaurat Schluter (marine engineer)
Leutnant zur See Schmidt
Oberleutnant zur See Sonntag

FLEET STAFF
Admiral Günther Lütjens (Fleet Commander)
Kapitän zur See Harald Netzband (Chief of Staff)
Kapitän zur See Paul Ascher (Admiral's Staff)
Kapitän zur See Emil Melms (Admiral's Staff)
Korvettenkapitän Hans Nitzschke (Admiral's Staff)
Fregattenkapitän Dipl-Ing Karl Thannemann (Fleet Engineer)
Dr Med Hans-Roleff Riege (Fleet Medical Officer)
Marineoberkriegsgerichtsrat Eduard Langer (Fleet Advocate)
Major Grohe (Luftwaffe Liaison Officer)

THE WORLD'S BATTLESHIP FLEETS COMPARED

GREAT BRITAIN

In 1936, faced not only with a potential threat to her possessions in the Far East, but also with one much closer to home from a revitalized and increasingly aggressive Germany and an ambitious Italy, Britain began to rearm. Five King George V class fast battleships of 35,561 tonnes (35,000 tons) were laid down, each armed with ten 355mm (14in) guns and 16 133mm (5.25in) dual-purpose guns. These were followed, after Japan had abandoned the Treaty limits, by four Lion-class ships of 40,642 tonnes (40,000 tons) mounting nine 406mm (16in) guns, although the Lions were later cancelled. At the same time, existing British capital ships were modernized with the provision of extra armour and improved armament. However, although four new battleships of the King George V class (*Prince of Wales*, *Duke of York*, *Anson* and *Howe*) were building at the start of 1939, none would be ready for at least 18 months; and of the 15 existing capital ships, only two, the *Nelson* and *Rodney*, had been built since 1918. Four of the five KGV class battleships survived the war; the fifth – the *Prince of Wales* – took part in the operation against the *Bismarck*, but was then sunk by Japanese air attack off Malaya on 10 December 1941.

King George V Class
Displacement: 36,725t standard, 42,075t full load
Dimensions: 227.05 x 31.40 x 9.95m (745 x 103 x 32ft 7in)
Machinery: four-shaft, Parsons geared turbines, 110,000hp
Speed: 28 knots
Range: 27,800km (15,000nm) at 10 knots
Armour: belt 380-356mm (15-13in); deck 140-25mm (5.5-1in); bulkheads 305-102mm (12-4in); barbettes 356mm (13in); turret faces 356mm (13in); conning tower 114mm (4.5in)
Armament: ten 35.6cm (14in); 16 13.5cm (5.25in); eight 40mm; 32 (later 88) 2pdr pom-poms; up to 64 20mm; two Supermarine Walrus aircraft
Complement: 1422

FRANCE

In the early 1930s, the French Navy's battleship fleet was in a sorry state. Of the older Courbet-class dreadnoughts, *Courbet* herself, *Jean Bart* and *Paris* all underwent reconstruction in 1927-31 and were subsequently used as training ships (the fourth ship of this class, *France*, had foundered in Quiberon Bay in August 1933, after striking a submerged rock). Three more modern dreadnoughts, the *Bretagne*, *Lorraine* and *Provence*, were undergoing a substantial refit in 1932-34; and four modern battleships, the *Richelieu*, *Strasbourg*, *Clemenceau* and *Jean Bart* (the older *Jean Bart* having been renamed *Océan*), were only laid down in 1935-38. Of the four, Clemenceau was never completed; *Jean Bart* was immobilized in Casablanca after the fall of France; *Strasbourg* was immobilized in Toulon; and *Richelieu* was under the Vichy flag at Dakar at the time of the *Bismarck* episode. Had she been serving with the Allies at the time, she would have been a fast and most powerful addition to the hunt for the German battleship. She later served with the British Eastern Fleet.

Richelieu Class
Displacement: 35,000t standard; 43,000t full load
Dimensions: 247.85 x 33 x 9.6m (813ft 2in x 108ft 3in x 31ft 3in)
Machinery: four-shaft, Parsons geared turbines, 150,000hp
Speed: 30 knots
Range: 27,800km (15,000nm)
Armour: belt 345-240mm (13.5-9.5in); bulkheads 380-240mm (15-9.5in); decks 150-50mm (6-2in); turret faces 445mm (17.5in); secondary armament 125mm (5in)
Armament: eight 38cm (15in); nine 152mm (6in); 12 100mm (3.9in) AA; eight 37mm; 48 20mm; 16 13.2mm MG
Complement: 1670

ITALY

Two of Italy's dreadnoughts dating from World War I, the *Conte di Cavour* and *Giulio Cesare*, were completely rebuilt in the early 1930s. In 1937 the *Andrea Doria* and *Caio Duilio* were also rebuilt. In the meantime, in response to the potential threat from France's Dunkerque class, the Italian Admiralty ordered the construction of a new class of battleship, the Vittorio Veneto. The class leader was laid down in 1934, together with a second ship, the *Littorio*; both were completed in 1940. A third vessel, the *Roma*, was not laid down until 1938 and was not completed until 1942. These were excellent, well-designed ships, fast and well armed. When France collapsed in June 1940, Italy's battleships were to present a formidable challenge to British naval superiority in the Mediterranean, but most were quickly disabled.

Vittorio Veneto Class
Displacement: 40,520t standard; 45,030t full load
Dimensions: 237.75 x 32.80 x 10.5m (780ft x 107ft 7in x 34ft 6in)
Machinery: four-shaft, Belluzo geared turbines, 128,200hp
Speed: 31 knots
Range: 8500km (4600nm)
Armour: belt 280mm (11in); bulkheads 210mm (8.25in); decks 162-45mm (6.4-1.8in); barbettes 350-280mm (13.8-11in); turret faces 350mm (13.8in); conning tower 260mm (10.2in)
Armament: nine 38cm (15in), 12 15.2cm (6in), four 12cm (4.7in); 12 8.9cm (3.5in) AA; 20 37mm; 16 20mm
Complement: 1830

JAPAN

In the 1930s, the Western powers had little idea of the true state of the Japanese Navy and its associated maritime air power, on which intelligence was almost completely lacking. In 1915, following disagreements between the USA and Japan over the latter's policies in China, the Japanese Navy had decided to build more battleships to attain parity with the Americans. The plan called for eight battleships and eight battlecruisers to be built by 1922.

In the event, as a result of the Washington Treaty, only the first two battleships were built and two more completed as aircraft carriers. The battleships were the *Nagato* and *Mutsu*, both of which were reconstructed in 1934–36. In 1937, in contravention of the various naval treaties, Japan initiated construction of the Yamato-class battleships, the largest and most powerful ever built. One vessel, the *Shinano*, was completed as an aircraft carrier, and a planned fourth ship was never built. The two remaining ships were the *Yamato* and *Musashi*; named after Japanese provinces, they were commissioned in 1942. Built in great secrecy, they were designed to compete on equal terms with any group of enemy battleships. The irony was that both were ultimately destroyed by the very weapon that brought Japan her early victories in the Pacific – naval air power. *Musashi* was sunk by US carrier aircraft in the Battle of Leyte Gulf, October 1944, while *Yamato* was sunk in similar fashion while making a 'kamikaze' sortie to Okinawa in April 1945.

Yamato Class
Displacement: 65,000t standard, 72,810t full load
Dimensions: 263m x 36.9m x 10.4m (862ft 9in x 121ft 1in x 34ft 1in)
Machinery: four-shaft, Kampon geared turbines, 150,000hp
Speed: 27 knots
Range: 13,320km (7200nm) at 16 knots
Armour: belt 410mm (16.1in); deck 230–200mm (9.1–7.9in); turret faces 650mm (25.6in); conning tower 500mm (19.7in)
Armament: nine 46cm (18.1in); 12 15.5cm (6.1in); 12 (later 24) 12.7cm (5in); 24 (later 150) 25mm; six or seven aircraft
Complement: 2500

THE UNITED STATES

By 1930, the United States Navy had attained a principal post-World War I goal, which was to achieve parity in capital ships with the Royal Navy. Fifteen battleships were in commission, all dreadnoughts, and all subject to major reconstruction and refitting programmes. Development continued with the North Carolina and South Dakota classes of 1937–38 (*North Carolina, Washington, Alabama, Indiana, Massachusetts* and *South Dakota*), ships of 35,562 tonnes (35,000 tons) and carrying a main armament of nine 406mm (16in) guns. These in turn were overshadowed by the Iowa class of 1939–40 (*Iowa, Missouri, New Jersey* and *Wisconsin*), displacing 48,000 tonnes (45,000 tons).

Iowa class
Displacement: 48,110t standard; 57,540t full load
Dimensions: 270.45 x 32.95 x 11m (887ft 3in x 108ft 2in x 36ft 2in)
Machinery: four-shaft, General Electric geared turbines, 212,000hp
Speed: 33 knots
Range: 27,800km (15,000nm) at 15 knots
Armour: belt 310mm (12.2in); deck 152mm (6in); bulkheads 280mm (11in); barbettes 440–287mm (17.3–11.3in); turret faces 500mm (19.7in); conning tower 440mm (17.3in)
Armament: nine 406mm (16in); 20 127mm (5in); 76 40mm; 52 20mm
Complement: 1921

THE FATE OF THE SUPPORT VESSELS AND SUBMARINES INVOLVED IN OPERATION RHEINÜBUNG

TANKERS

Belchen: sunk by British cruisers *Aurora* and *Kenya* between Greenland and Labrador, 3 June 1941

Egerland: intercepted by British naval forces and scuttled off Freetown, Sierra Leone, 5 June 1941

Esso Hamburg: intercepted by cruiser HMS *London* and destroyer HMS *Brilliant* in central Atlantic and scuttled, 5 June 1941

Friedrich Breme: intercepted by HMS *Sheffield* west-northwest of Cape Finisterre, 12 June 1941, and scuttled

Heide: recovered to French port

Lothringen: captured by HMS *Dunedin* in central Atlantic, 15 June 1941

Weissenburg: recovered to French port

SUPPLY SHIPS

Alstertor: intercepted by British naval force and scuttled off Cape Finisterre, 20 June 1941

Gedania: captured by Royal Navy, 4 June 1941

Spichern: recovered to French port

PATROL SHIPS

Gonzenheim: intercepted by battleship HMS *Nelson* and cruiser HMS *Neptune* and scuttled, 4 June 1941

Kota Pinang: recovered to French port; sunk west of Cape Finisterre by cruiser HMS *Kenya*, 3 October 1941

WEATHER SHIPS

August Wriedt: sunk in Arctic by Royal Navy, 29 May 1941

Hinrich Freese: sunk in Arctic by Royal Navy, 29 May 1941

Lauenberg: destroyed by British naval forces near Jan Mayen Island, 28 June 1941

München: captured by Royal Navy, 7 May 1941

ESCORT VESSELS

Friedrich Eckoldt: sunk by RN cruisers HMS *Sheffield* and *Jamaica* in Battle of the Barents Sea, 31 December 1942

Hans Lody: to RN as *R38*, 1945; broken up 1949

Sperrbrecher 13: scuttled, May 1945

Sperrbrecher 31: scuttled, May 1945

Z23: bombed and sunk at La Pallice, 21 August 1944

SUBMARINES

Barbarigo (Italian): sunk by air attack in Bay of Biscay, 19 June 1943

U43: sunk by US carrier aircraft southwest of Azores, 30 July 1943

U46: scuttled at Neustadt, 4 May 1945

U48: scuttled at Neustadt, 4 May 1945

U66: sunk by US carrier aircraft off Cape Verde, 6 May 1944

U73: sunk off Oran by US destroyers, 16 December 1943

U74: sunk by RN destroyers off Cartagena, 2 May 1942

U93: sunk off Madeira by RN destroyer *Hesperus*, 15 January 1942

U94: sunk in Caribbean by RCN *Oakville* and aircraft, 28 August 1942

U97: bombed and sunk off Haifa, 16 June 1943

U98: bombed and sunk off Gibraltar, 19 November 1942

U556: sunk southwest of Iceland by RN corvettes, 27 June 1941

U557: lost in collision with Italian MTB off Salamis, 16 December 1941

THE FATE OF ALLIED WARSHIPS INVOLVED IN THE HUNT FOR THE BISMARCK

AIRCRAFT CARRIERS

Ark Royal: torpedoed by the *U81* in the Mediterranean and sank under tow, 14 November 1941

Eagle: sunk by U73 north of Algiers, 11 August 1942

Victorious: scrapped at Faslane, July 1969

BATTLESHIPS

King George V: scrapped at Dalmuir and Troon, 1958-59

Nelson: scrapped at Inverkeithing, 1949

Prince of Wales: sunk by Japanese air attack off Malaya, 10 December 1941

Ramillies: scrapped at Cairn Ryan and Troon, 1948-49

Rodney: scrapped at Inverkeithing, 1948

BATTLECRUISERS

Hood: sunk by gunfire from Bismarck south of Greenland, 24 May 1941

Renown: scrapped at Faslane, 1948

Repulse: sunk by Japanese air attack off Malaya, 10 December 1941

CRUISERS

Arethusa: scrapped at Troon, 1950

Aurora: to Nationalist China, 1948. Seized by Communists; sunk March 1949 and later salvaged. Scrapped in 1950s

Birmingham: scrapped at Inverkeithing, 1960

Dorsetshire: sunk by Japanese air attack off Ceylon, 5 April 1942

Edinburgh: torpedoed in Barents Sea by *U456* and destroyers; scuttled 2 May 1942

Galatea: sunk off Alexandria by *U557*, 15 December 1941

Hermione: sunk south of Crete by *U205*, 16 June 1942

Kenya: scrapped at Faslane, 1962

London: scrapped at Barrow, 1950

Manchester: torpedoed by Italian MTBs off Tunisia and scuttled, 13 August 1942

Norfolk: scrapped at Newport, 1950

Sheffield: scrapped at Inverkeithing, 1967

Suffolk: scrapped at Newport, 1948

DESTROYERS

Achates: sunk by Admiral Hipper in Barents Sea, 31 December 1942

Active: scrapped at Troon, 1947

Antelope: scrapped at Blyth, 1946

Anthony: scrapped at Troon, 1948

Cossack: sunk by *U563*, N. Atlantic, 27 October 1941

Echo: scrapped at Dunston, 1956

Electra: sunk in Battle of Java Sea, 27 August 42

Faulknor: scrapped at Milford Haven, 1946

Foresight: sunk by enemy aircraft in Mediterranean, 13 August 1942

Forester: scrapped at Rosyth, 1947

Foxhound: to RCN as *Qu'appelle*, 1944; scrapped 1948

Fury: mined off Normandy, 21 June 1944; deemed a constructive total loss and scrapped at Briton Ferry, September 1944

Hesperus: broken up, 1946

Icarus: scrapped at Troon, 1947

Inglefield: sunk by air attack of Anzio, 25 February 1944

Intrepid: sunk off Leros by air attack, 27 September 1943

Lance: bombed at Malta 22 October 1942 and deemed a constructive total loss; scrapped, June 1944

Maori: sunk by air attack, Malta, 12 February 1942

Mashona: bombed and sunk southwest of Ireland by FW200, 28 May 1941

Piorun (Polish): formerly HMS *Nerissa*. Returned to UK and scrapped, 1946

Punjabi: lost in collision with *KGV*, N. Atlantic, 1 May 1942

Sikh: sunk by shore batteries at Tobruk, 14 September 1942

Somali: sunk by *U703* south of Iceland, 24 September 1942

Tartar: scrapped at Newport, 1948

Zulu: sunk by enemy air attack off Tobruk, 14 September 1942

INDEX

Page references in italics refer to illustration captions